Nevada Military Place Names
of the
Indian Wars and Civil War

Charles McDermit, commander of
Fort Churchill
Courtesy: Nevada Historical Society

Nevada Military Place Names
of the
Indian Wars and Civil War

Daniel C. B. Rathbun

Yucca Tree Press

First Printing   January 2002

Rathbun, Daniel C. B.
    Nevada Military Place Names of the Indian Wars and Civil War.
    1. Nevada - History.   2. Indian Wars.   3. Civil War - Nevada.
    4. Fortifications - Military.   5. U.S. Army - Cavalry.
    6. Nevada - Guidebooks
    I. Daniel C.B. Rathbun.   II. Title

ISBN: 1-881325-51-2
Library of Congress Control Number: 2001098553

Cover Design: Stephen Matson
Cover Photo: Soldiers, Fort McDermit, c. 1877
        Courtesy: University of Nevada - Reno Library

Soon with angels I'll be marching
With bright laurels on my brow,
I have for my country fallen.
Who will care for Mother now?

from *"Who Will Care for
Mother Now?"*
Charles Carroll Sacoyer, 1863

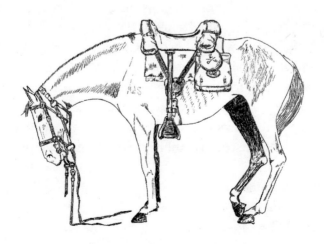

Acknowledgments

Special thanks are extended to all of the librarians, records managers, archivists, curators, military post historians, cadastral surveyors, etc. There was always at least one person—and many times there were several people—in libraries, museums, public facilities and historical societies who willingly stopped whatever else they were doing to befriend my efforts. They would ferret out obscure books, pamphlets, maps, photographs, special collections, and all of the other documents that went into the accounts documented here. To specifically list them by name would read like the muster rolls of a small company. Their organizations include the Nevada Historical Society, the State Archives, and the Special Collections unit at the Getchell Library, University of Nevada-Reno. Without their help and encouragement I would still be wandering through the stacks of the first library, blankly looking at the spines of a thousand books.

In addition, thanks go to the countless private land owners and other 'locals' who volunteered information, directions, and access, or otherwise facilitated the efforts in the field throughout Nevada. Their appreciation for the land, its history and its heritage was a pleasure to experience and should never be underestimated.

For their review and encouragement I thank Dr. Michael Brodhead, University of Nevada-Reno, Mr. Clyde Murray, my neighbor and major; and Pat Barker, BLM State Archeologist for Nevada. Their unmericiful, critical review was invaluable.

My special thanks to Janie Matson for her patience, editing, suggestions and advice in assembling and publishing the final product.

Daniel C.B. Rathbun
Reno, Nevada
January 2002

Table of Contents

List of Illustrations

FOREWORD

Surprisingly little has been written about the conflict between the Indians of Nevada and the new settlers. There is a general public awareness of the pioneers' crossing, discovery of the Comstock lode, development of agriculture and the evolution of the entertainment and gaming industry, but the knowledge of the early human conflict seems limited to the battles near Pyramid Lake and a vague awareness of the military garrison at Fort Churchill. Missing is an understanding of the intense struggle between cultures with conflicting values, varying customs, differing technology and unrelated objectives. The story of the interaction is a fascinating mosaic that both reaffirms the fundamental character and diversity of human nature and reinforces the value of history's lessons in anticipating the future. The down side of such study is that history is most frequently recorded and published by the victor, not the vanquished. As a result, many of the tales here are admittedly from a white, rather than Indian perspective. This is not to diminish the Indian view, but more a reflection of the availability of literature and the attitudes of early authors.

The most reliable documented source is the official military records. Actual correspondence, orders, reports of expeditions, unit and post returns, published regulations and other documents are available, replete with meticulous detail. To prepare this text, information from these documents was entered into a data base recording the who, what, when, where, and source. Information from the history works of Myron Angel (Thompson and West - 1881) and Hubert Bancroft (1890) was added to the data base. Newspaper accounts of the times were then added along with other more recent works. By sorting the lines of data either according to date or the unit involved or other factors such as the unit commander, officers, non-commissioned officers or location a very complete picture emerged. Any contradictions or omissions in the data became glaringly apparent and could usually be reconciled by further search. Much of the text lets the facts tell the story. However, quotations (sometimes biased, colorful and occasionally offensive by modern standards) add the mood, language and thoughts of the time.

A great challenge was found in correctly placing the event on the ground. Maps of the time were good. But, the lack of geographic names, combined with changing names, inaccurate estimates of distance, varying levels of both penmanship and literacy all contributed to the difficulty of the search. The most reliable source of geographic names is the plats and field notes of the early cadastral* surveyors of the General Land Office. Using instruments we would regard as crude and primitive, maps of amazing accuracy were created by the U.S. Topographical Engineers and the cadastral surveyors. When held to standards now available through satellite technology and Global Positioning Systems, the accuracy of early maps is not flawless, but is truly amazing in its quality.

If location was the greatest challenge, it also held the greatest reward. Countless hours were spent reviewing the plats and notes of these surveyors in search of geographic names. The thrill of finding a particular spring or certain station on a surveyor's plat is on a par with actually finding the rock outline of a foundation on the ground. The collective reward was a set of locations that are indisputably accurate and in some cases heretofore seemingly lost to the current record.

---

* A public record of the extent, value, and ownership of land for taxation purposes.

FOR MEXICO DIRECT!

...AND...

THE UNION FOREVER.

—

I WANT TWENTY-TWO NON-COMISS-
ioned Officers and sixty privates to make up
my company of Mounted Infantry, Company D
First Regiment Nevada Territory Volunteers, to
be mustered into the service of the United States
immediately. Subsistence and clothing furnished as soon as enrolled.

$100 BOUNTY GUARANTEED

by the laws of the United States, and five dollars
per month by Nevada Territory, in addition to
the regular pay.

☞ Recruiting Office at F. J. HAMMELL'S
ORIGINAL SALOON, No. 51 South C street.

E. B. BLAKE,
Captain Co. D, Mounted Infantry, First Reg'
N. T. Volunteers.   jan26 tf

Territorial Governor James W. Nye.
Courtesy: Special Collections,
University of Nevada-Reno Library

INTRODUCTION

The Environment

Early travelers in Nevada usually followed the California Emigrant Trail, the Overland Trail or the Old Spanish Trail. Today, cross-country travelers experience the same vistas along Interstate 80, US Highway 50 and Interstate 15, respectively. Not without some truth, light-hearted Nevadans warn visitors to watch for signs a mile on either side of the Interstate highways, "Entering Nevada—Set Watch Back 100 Years." Other than the urban areas around Reno, Las Vegas, Elko, and a few mines very, little has changed from the early landscape.

These roads follow the path of least resistance across the basins and as a result the land appears harsh, dry and uninviting; largely vacant and devoid of vegetation over waist-high. Until one is within sight of the Sierra Nevadas, streams are almost non-existent. The few streams that one sees disappear into barren playas or closed saline basins. Residents joke that coyotes carry canteens and rabbits pack a lunch. This seems to be an accurate depiction, particularly in the winter. However, in the warmer months the hidden reality stands in stark contrast to the view from the highway. Within the mountains and foothills are literally thousands of springs, countless miles of small streams, millions of acres woodlands, numerous aspen groves and an abundance small game that provide life's physical as well as spiritual needs. When properly gathered and stored, the harvest was capable of sustaining the large native population even through the bleak winter months.

If in fact you could 'set your watch back one hundred years,' or more accurately one hundred and fifty years, you would find the same physical environment. What would be different would be the human component of the environment. You would find people of two diverse cultures interacting for the first time; each struggling to achieve or maintain their individual and collective objectives, each following their traditional ways.

The Indians

Indians of historic Nevada were linked mainly by language, custom, practices and lifestyle and were lumped into the Shoshonean linguistic group. They were represented by various bands of the Paiutes, Bannocks, and Western Shoshone. Several alternate or sub-cultural names appear in more detailed literature. Politically, there was no central authority, but councils of the chiefs were common. Consensus was sometimes obtained in these councils, but not believed to be a requirement. Subdivision of tribes took the form of separate bands with respective territories generally defined by custom and habitual occupation. Migration and marriage of individuals between tribes and territories was common. Small extended family groups roamed widely following seasonal production of pine nuts, grasses and small game. They shared readily and would occasionally unite to hunt or for harvest. Some gatherings of family groups formed small villages around permanent lakes and along perennial streams. They believed in an afterlife and a higher order of spirits related to the land, the flora and fauna, seasons and natural phenomena.

The Bannocks lived along what is now the Nevada-Oregon border and frequently co-mingled and even intermarried with the northern Paiutes. The Paiutes were geographically the largest group. In the mid-1800's the northern Paiutes and related Washoes occupied western Nevada from the Sierra Front east to the Desatoya Mountain Range. Southern Paiutes lived in the Pahranagut Valley south to the bend of the Colorado River. The Shoshones filled the northeastern corner of the state from the Humboldt River north, as well as the area between the Desatoya Range east to the to the Cherry Creek and Egan Ranges. The Goshutes, a hybrid of Utes, Shoshones and Paiutes, used the area north of the Pahranagut Valley and east of the Egan and Cherry Creek Ranges. Although not absolute, these generalized territories reliably match the literature and events of the time.

The sparse and inhospitable environment of the Great Basin made the Paiutes a gentle, self reliant, resourceful culture; greatly adapted to their environment; and prone to withdraw rather than confront more aggressive and better armed enemies. Initially, they were not prone toward hostility with the whites. However, this changed with time and the Paiutes produced some of the fiercest fighting in the Great Basin, particularly by tribal renegades.

Of the Shoshones and other tribes Indian Agent Garland Hurt wrote in 1860, "the To-si-witches (White Knives) inhabiting the Humboldt River ... are a very treacherous people; and the Bannacks, Go-sha-Utes, and Cum-um-pahs are not much less so. These latter bands are in the habit of infesting the emigration-road between Soda Springs and the Bear River and the head of the Humboldt, during the season of emigration to California; it is believed, and I think, not without plausible foundation, that persons residing within the settlements of Utah encourage these spoliations by offering a market for the property thus obtained."[1]

According to Captain John C. Fremont, U.S. Topographical Engineers, in 1859, the Goshutes "are an offshoot of the Ute Indians, and are the offspring of a disaffected portion of this tribe, that left their nation about two generations ago, under their leader or chief Go-ship, and hence the name Go-ship-Ute, since contracted into Go-shutes."[2] He further describes a very meager existence for the Goshutes.

The primary focus of each group was meeting the minimum requirements of food, shelter and mere survival rather than a higher goal of preserving an ideology. The arrival of whites brought the horse, firearms, and competition for the limited natural resources. The most radical changes in the Indian life style occurred during the 1850s, radiating out from the emigrant routes and mining towns. The Indians desired to avoid the whites, but concurrently they quickly acquired a taste for white goods. Gatherings of Indian family groups became more frequent and enduring. Pyramid Lake and Walker Lake became areas of concentration. The balance of power of one Indian group over another was tipped in favor of those with horses and firearms. Conflicts between Paiutes and Shoshones became more pronounced.

As a whole the Indians seemed to have no specific agenda relative to the whites. Interaction seemed to be motivated more by a desire to acquire goods and to exist peacefully rather than any other social factor. In 1859 Dr. I. Forney, Superintendent of Indian Affairs in Utah (including present-day Nevada), estimated populations at 4,500 'Sho-sho-nees' (including 200-300 Goshutes), 500 'Bannacks,' 2,200 'Pey-Utes (South),' 6000 'Pey-Utes (West),' and 700 'Wa-sho of Honey Lake.'[3]

Prior to 1860 acts of Indian aggression were usually linked either to retaliation for white aggression or specific mistreatment; acquisition of food or material goods for survival or to be traded in Utah; or lack of understanding of white law and social custom. By 1860, demand for the scant resources of the Great Basin reached a breaking point. A council of Paiute Indian chiefs was held at Pyramid Lake to debate war. Although they were split, the meeting precipitated attacks by Paiutes and Bannocks that cast the die in May 1860. Conflict escalated, reaching its peak in 1865. Throughout the period the Indian population was divided between those desiring a peaceful coexistence and those prone to war. The majority of the warring groups were coalitions of renegades from the Modoc, Bannock, Paiute and Western Shoshone tribes.

The Settlers

At the conclusion of the War with Mexico in 1848, all of what is now California and Nevada became part of the United States. That same year the discovery of gold accelerated the westward movement of gold seekers and settlers. Between 1849 and 1852 an estimated 120,000 immigrants traveled across Nevada en route to California. The earliest permanent white settlements were Mormon stations along the trails. In general, the Mormons got along well with the Indians. However, prospecting and discovery of rich mineral deposits in western Nevada, combined with Brigham Young's recall of the Mormons to Utah in 1857, changed the character of the white culture. Nearly all of the Mormon stations were taken over by other whites who were either indifferent toward the Indians or exploited or abused them. Miners usually ignored the Indians or dealt with them as an impediment to development of mineral resources and commerce along the trails. With mining came cultivation, ranching and additional commerce. The best farming and grazing lands were also the most fertile areas for the Indians seed and game harvest. Conflicts became more frequent. A major Indian defeat of a white force near Pyramid Lake introduced the military into the Great Basin. Public sentiment toward Indians was generally condescending and intolerant.

The Military

Three types of military units operated during the Indian Wars: the United States Army, the California and Nevada volunteer units, and civilian militia units.

United States Army. The early role of the U.S. Army in Nevada was exploration and reporting. Captain John C. Fremont and later Captain James Hervey Simpson, both of the U.S. Army's Topographical Engineers documented the trails and resources of the area. Not until 1860 was a field unit of the U.S. Army permanently garrisoned in Nevada. After the second battle near Pyramid Lake their role was more as a police force and deterrent than an arm of aggression. Led by career officers, many of them West Point graduates, the Army seemed to have no particular agenda other than maintenance of order including prevention and punishment of aggression. Their presence was active, but was soon interrupted by the Civil War. Other than the command at the Department of the Pacific in San Francisco, regular troops were absent from Western states and territories from late 1861 to early 1866. In 1866 regular units began returning to Nevada. Arriving near the end of the uprising of 1865, the majority of their activity was against remnant bands of renegades known to have committed depredations.

Volunteer Cavalry and Infantry. Between late 1861 and mid-1866 volunteer units mustered into Federal service filled the military role. Officers and members were recruited from the civilian population in California and Nevada. Many of the leaders were veterans of the War with Mexico and several officers held elected public office prior to service in the volunteer force. Their attitudes toward Indians were shaped by personal experiences as pioneer civilians and the popular public sentiment. These responses ranged from strongly anti-Indian to a more neutral sense of duty and public service to uphold treaties and agreements. In nearly all combat these soldiers were unmerciful toward warring Indians and, as a minimum, tolerant of non-combatent Indians. Conversely, on many occasions they were not only sympathetic, but also supportive of Indians' needs in adminis-tration of agreements with the white civilian authorities. How-ever, egregious exceptions dot the history.

In October 1861, numerous volunteers from Carson City, Virginia City, Dayton and Reno were recruited into volunteer units formed in California. Although designated as Company F, 2nd California Infantry, the unit was actually recruited and organized in Carson City, Nevada, by Captain Charles D. Douglas. California units serving in northern Nevada included the 2nd California Cavalry, and the 2nd, 3rd and 6th California Infantry. In 1863, officers for the Nevada volunteers were locally recruited and then trained and certified to U.S. Army standards at Fort Churchill. Newly certified Captains then recruited unit members locally. They were then equipped, trained, supplied and regulated by the U. S. Army. Two battalion-sized units were formed and designated as the 1st Nevada Cavalry and 1st Nevada Infantry. These units were part of the Military Department of California and served in several western states and territories, primarily Nevada, Utah and Wyoming. Many of the camps and forts identified in this book were established and manned by these California and Nevada volunteers. The last organized Nevada volunteer unit was mustered out of Federal service on July 21, 1866. These Nevada and California volunteer units began the lineage of Nevada and California Army and Air National Guard units in service today.

Militia. At various times in Nevada's early history there were groups of armed citizens organized along military lines and referred to as 'Militia.' They often served using their personal firearms, equipment and uniforms. In general they were untrained, lacked discipline and performed poorly. Officers for such units were either elected or appointed based on political influence or economic status. Unless called in support of an Army unit, members usually served without pay. Occasionally they were modestly subsidized by local government or gratuitously by local businesses. They often had localized names such as the Virginia Blues, Washoe Rifles, Lander Blues and others. While some individual members may have been skilled in military arts, collectively the militia was usually more of a threat to themselves in the field than to the hostile segment of the Indian population. Their often inept, prejudiced, indiscriminate and unfocused approach did more to aggravate or prolong hostility than to subdue hostile factions and promote a peaceful co-existence.

Paradise Valley .

Winnemucca .

Gerlach .

Battle Mtn

. Elko

. Reno

. Fallon

. Austin

Eureka

. Ely

. Carson City

NEVADA
Location Map

. Las Vegas

HOW TO USE THIS BOOK

Sites are listed alphabetically. Most site descriptions include the site name, the County and the who, what, when, where and why to the extent they are known. Casualties and effects are also indicated. Information is arranged as follows:

Site Name
County

Description of the activity at the site usually includes name and rank of the senior players; the unit designation or tribal affiliation; the date of the event; the intent of the action, and the general results. If the site includes a structure, the current condition and land status are indicated.

The last paragraph gives a narrative description of how to reach the site from the nearest town shown on the Official State of Nevada highway map. Highway numbers are those shown in the *Nevada Atlas and Gazetteer* published by DeLorme.

A word about etiquette and rules

Many of the sites are located on private land, Indian trust land or reservation lands. Local inquiry will often lead to the owner's name. A phone call prior to visiting a landowner's home is a common courtesy and says a lot to the owner about your attitude and likely behavior if permission is given for your visit. A polite and respectful approach can often gain permission for you to visit the site. Once on the site leave your shovels, metal detectors, screens or whatever either at home or in your vehicle. If you bring a lunch or make a camping trip out of your visit obtain permission first. Plan to bring your own drinking water. If you want a camp fire (not recommended) ask permission, check the fire danger and bring your own wood. Stay away from livestock facilities—particularly water sources—pack out everything you bring in and respect the area as though it was your own back yard—better yet, respect it as though it was your front yard. Stay on existing roads and trails. If they are muddy you would be smart to pick another day for your visit.

If the site is on public land these same general rules apply. It is always wise to make inquiry at the local Field Office of the Bureau of Land Management. You will usually find someone whose interests coincide with yours and who is familiar with the sites, current road conditions and the best way to get there. They will give you the current status of any fire restrictions and can usually suggest a better place to camp than what you would find on your own. Maps at 1:100,000 are for sale in BLM offices and are very useful for navigation.

Remember, there is no such thing as 'finders-keepers' on either private or public lands. In the case of public lands there are penalties for disturbing or removing almost every man-made object you discover. Leave the site like you find it so the next person will have the same level of enjoyment you have experienced. If you observe recent damage, tell the BLM about it.

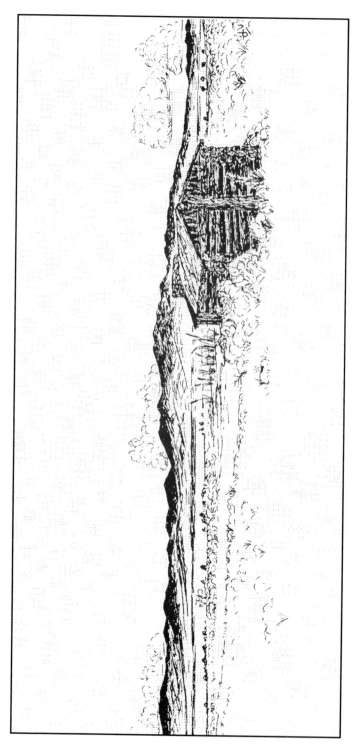

View to the east from Antelope Springs Station.
Courtesy: The Author

ALPHABETICAL ENTRIES FOR SITES

Antelope Springs Station/Antelope Wells
White Pine County

Called 'Kwadumba' (antelope water) by the Indians, Antelope Springs was an important stop on the Overland Trail between Camp Floyd, Utah, and Genoa, Nevada.[1] It first served the Holladay Overland Mail and Express Company in 1854. When Holladay lost the mail contract the station was taken over by the Overland Stage.[2] By 1860 the site served the Pony Express as well. Located in the heart of Goshute Indian country, it was frequently raided. Beginning in the late 1850's military patrols frequently visited the site. After it was burned by Indians in June 1860, a small contingent of soldiers from Utah was assigned here. The soldiers were removed at the beginning of the Civil War.

Its strategic location on the Overland Trail brought the military back in the spring of 1862. It was used regularly by transient military units and supply trains between Camp Ruby and Camp Floyd, Utah. From 1863 to 1865, a minimum of four or five infantry soldiers were garrisoned here to protect the station. The station was abandoned in 1869 when the transcontinental railroad became the primary means for cross country commerce.[3]

Go thirty-seven miles north from Ely on US 93 to Schellbourne. Take State Route 2 to the east ten and one half miles through the pass to State Route 893. Go south slightly over three miles to a junction (look for a large stone house) where you turn east continuing on State Route 2. The road winds through foothills almost five more miles to another junction. Turn toward the northeast and continue approximately eight and one half miles toward the Tippett Ranch. The site of the Antelope Springs Station is on private land approximately one and one half miles west of this point. Only the rock outline of the station foundation remains. A steel post, dedicated in June 2001, marks the exact location of the building.[4]

Applegate-Lassen Trail
Churchill, Humboldt and Washoe Counties

Established by Jesse Applegate and Peter Lassen in 1846, the trail was a spur from the California Emigrant Trail. The spur left the Emigrant Trail in the vicinity of Mill City (exit 151 on I-80). It crossed the Humboldt River near Saint Mary's (above Rye Patch Reservoir) and continued across the Black Rock Desert, ultimately ending near Goose Lake in California. Stations along the trail during the Indian Wars include Saint Mary's, Willow Springs, Rabbit Hole, Soldier Meadows, and Massacre Lake. The trail has been commemorated with a series of 'T'-shaped railroad rail markers put in place by the Oregon-California Trail Association.

Aurora
Mineral County

A mining camp established in August 1860, Aurora is only four miles from the California-Nevada boundary. For a while it was thought to actually be in California. As a result, it has served as county seat for both Esmeralda County in Nevada and Mono County in California. The town peaked at approximately 5000 residents, one of whom was Mark Twain.[5]

'Camp Aurora'[6] refers to undescribed meeting places of the Aurora Militia and to temporary camp sites used by transient military units passing through the area. Camp Aurora has also been used to refer to a site in Adobe Meadows, California, occupied by Company A, 2nd California Cavalry, from May to August 1862. Captain Edwin A. Rowe commanded the company and came to the area in response to requests for protection against marauding Indians southwest of the town. Rowe, working together with Indian Agent Warren Wasson succeeded in gaining peace with the Indians in the area under Chief George.[7]

By April 1863, exploration by miners and Indian depredation prompted Wasson to revisit Aurora. His mission was to meet with eastern California Indians near Mono Lake and in the Owens River Valley; determine the nature of their troubles with the whites; and seek resolution, if possible. He was accompanied by First

Lieutenant Herman Noble and fifty troopers of Company A, 2nd California Cavalry, from Fort Churchill. About halfway between Aurora and Owens Lake, Wasson encountered Lieutenant Colonel George Evans, Commander of the 2nd California Cavalry. Evans was accompanied by forty soldiers and an additional forty area citizens under California Militia Colonel William Mayfield. Evans and Mayfield were intent on avenging recent deaths in California from Indian depredations and wanted no part of Wasson's peacemaking. They believed that if peace was to be had, it would be had by killing all of the Indians involved in the deaths.[8] Far more compassionate, Wasson believed that the Owens River Indians had been pushed far enough. They had already been driven from their traditional use areas on the west side of the Sierra Nevada range. The Indians were now living on lands designated by the whites for their use and lacking any other option, they were prepared to defend this area to their death. The severe winter of 1862-63 led some of their band to steal livestock and raid whites. Wasson believed this was the source of the conflict and peaceful resolution was possible. Being in California, Wasson lacked the authority to pursue a peace treaty. Evans continued his search for the Indians until they were found near the Nevada-California boundary. Intent on a fight, he got one. In the battle the Indian's superior knowledge of the area, combined with excellent use of cover and concealment, allowed them to force the soldiers into retreat. Mayfield was killed and Private Thomas Spratt of Company G, 2nd California Cavalry, was wounded by a gunshot to the head in the first engagement. In a second engagement, Sergeant Christopher Gillespie of Company A under Noble was killed.[9] Evans eventually returned to his garrison near Los Angeles without achieving success in the field.[10]

The defeat, combined with the friction between Wasson and Evans, precipitated a meeting between Governor James W. Nye of Nevada, Governor Leland Stanford of California, General George Wright, Commander of the Department of the Pacific, California Indian Agent J.P.H. Wentworth and Wasson. Following the meeting Wasson and Wentworth meet with the Owens River

Indians and succeeded in securing a treaty closing the Owens River Indian War. The concerns in Aurora were set aside. Whites reduced incursions into lands designated for Indian use and depredation subsided. Indian-white problems were few and those were handled as civil matters involving individuals until 1864.[11] New mineral discoveries late that year increased white activity in the Indian areas and the number of incidents began to grow. This prompted the Aurora officials to again ask for a military post in January 1865.[12] (*See* Fish Lake.)

Aurora was also the scene of non-Indian military activity. In August 1862, Lieutenant Noble was in Aurora recovering from an illness. A group of secessionists, aware of both his presence and his poor health, decided to test the order that all military officers were obliged to arrest anyone speaking out against the Union. Boisterous toasts were made to Jefferson Davis, Stonewall Jackson and the Confederacy. Noble's troops were camped at Adobe Meadows. With their captain several miles away, Noble was alone. Local militia officers volunteered to muster a force to facilitate the arrests. This was done and the lieutenant, in the company of eleven militia, went to the house of the most outspoken antagonist. There they arrested Augustus Quinton. The sheriff, an elected official, refused to allow Quinton to be placed in his jail. The prisoner was then taken to the militia powder magazine. Other secessionists quickly armed themselves and a much bigger fight was now in the offing. The rest of the militia was called to arms. Faced with the possibility of a fight the secessionists backed down. Early the next morning, prisoner Quinton was marched to the flag pole. Here Noble administered the oath of allegiance, which Quinton quickly affirmed. The lieutenant was given three cheers by the locals followed by three cheers for the Stars and Stripes.[13] Other than civil matters, the area remained orderly for the remainder of the Civil War.

In 1865 a Private Sears deserted from one of the 1st Nevada Cavalry companies operating in Utah. He moved to Aurora where he was soon discovered. In April, Captain John G. Kelly, commander of Company C, 1st Nevada Infantry, arrested Sears.

Also in April 1865, notice of the Confederate surrender stirred A.C. Judy, a southern sympathizer, to speak out against the Union. Kelly, like Noble, used the local militia to arrest Judy. He promptly took the oath of allegiance and was released.[14]

The Aurora townsite is remote. There are no direct routes. It can be reached from Hawthorne, Nevada, by taking State Route 359 south. A little over three miles south of Hawthorne turn off State Route 359 to the west (toward the mountains) on Lucky Boy Pass Road. The road climbs up and over the mountain, through Lucky Boy Pass (approximately eight miles) and then descends into a large valley. At almost twelve miles there is an intersection with Forest Road 26. Don't take it; this is just a check point so you will know you are on the right road. Continue to the west nearly three miles to where Forest Road 58 takes off to the south. This is just another check point. To confirm your location you should see a north-south power line. Continue west for about two more miles to an intersection. Turn left (south). In about a mile you enter a canyon and the quality of the road deteriorates. Watch out for mine trucks. At six miles from the road back to Hawthorne, you are in the heart of the Aurora Mining District.

This is a good weather only adventure. Like many of the remote sites, you really have to want to go here to make this trip. It can be fun if you are well prepared and an impossible nightmare if you are not. If the road is wet, snow-covered or icy you should not make this trip even with four-wheel drive. The land is a mixture of both private and public land. Scattered private land and numerous mining claims limit public access in the area. Only foundations, broken glass and rusting metal remain at the Aurora townsite.

Adobe Meadows is in California approximately twenty-five miles south of the Aurora townsite.[15] It is northeast of Benton, California along California State Route 120.

Austin
Lander County
Located in the center of the Toiyabe Range, the site and its canyon were originally named 'Pony' by the riders of the Pony

Express. Although not on the official pony express route, many of the riders used the canyon to avoid Indian trouble or as an alternate route in bad weather. Discovery of silver in 1863 quickly generated a town of approximately 10,000. The name, Austin, is attributed to a variety of sources, including the capitol of Texas and commemoration of several different Nevada pioneers by that name.[16] Austin is first mentioned in a military context in 1863. Captain Noyes Baldwin passed through the town on 10 October 1863 leading newly formed Companies A and B, 1st Nevada Cavalry, to their permanent assignment at Camp Douglas, Utah Territory.[17]

On several occasions local citizens requested a garrison of troops for Austin. Lacking serious Indian problems they fell back on the popular theme of a looming Confederate take over. During his march to Fort Ruby in the summer of 1864 Captain George Alva Thurston was wined and dined and convinced to endorse a troop request to General Patrick Edward Connor in Utah. Connor provided a second endorsement and the request went on to General George Wright in California, commanding the Department of the Pacific. General Wright appropriately denied it for lack of sufficient justification or priority.[18]

Undaunted by the denial and still influenced by Austin's hospitality, on 26 November, Thurston sent Lieutenant John Tolles to follow up. Tolles' task was to investigate and document rumors of an Indian outbreak in the area and to confiscate any military clothing or equipment he might find in the possession of local citizens. Accompanied by Privates Jared Grover and I. Graham, Sergeant James H. Sanborn, and Drummer John E. Howe, the lieutenant camped at the Oregon Mill. From there he set about his investigation. The lieutenant's second task proved to be the more meaningful. Tolles found a local citizen with military clothing. The *Reese River Reveille* reported he "throttled a fellow who swore he was a border ruffian, and dared the officer to take from him a soldier's overcoat, which he was sporting. Said coat came off."[19] Tolles enjoyed the comforts of Austin, endeared himself to the local press and returned to Camp Ruby with a report that favored stationing troops there. The *Reese River Reveille* further courted the military officers with a story on the beleaguered conditions of "The Poor Soldier."[20] Lacking any real Indian threat against a town of several thousand; Austin's request for a garrison of troops was again denied. A militia was eventually established and named the Lander Blues.[21] Although they lacked equipment and expertise they at least satisfied the social need for a military presence in a time when patriotism and service were the theme of the day.

In early April 1865, Indian uprisings throughout the Northern Great Basin precipitated a genuine need for the military in rural areas adjacent to nearly every central Nevada settlement. Austin was no exception. In May, Thurston dispatched Lieutenant William G. Seamonds and Lieutenant Tolles with forty soldiers from Company B, 1st Nevada Infantry, to Austin. Their arrival was met with great fanfare and they quickly established a camp in the Upper Austin area. Each soldier was fully outfitted and the column contained several wagons, a surgeon and forty days' rations. There was even a mountain howitzer and wagon, complete with both round and grape shot and pulled by two six-mule teams. Fifty of the Lander Blues greeted them with appropriate ceremony. Several days later when the troops prepared to move to Gravelly Ford, where a major Indian gathering was reported, the fifty Lander Blues members faded into the population and did not accompany the troops.[22]

After Governor Henry G. Blasdel denied Seamonds request to order the Lander Blues into state service, Thurston ordered Seamonds to remain in the Austin area. No fool, Seamonds obeyed his orders and then proudly paraded his troops from their camp in Upper Austin through the streets of Austin and on to Clifton (near the present-day rodeo grounds) at the bottom of the western canyon. His march passed the offices of the *Reese River Reveille* where a military salute was offered.

On 29 May, Tolles and soldiers, now camped at Silver Creek, skirmished with three Indians caught in the act of stealing cattle from a local ranch. The Indians, two of them mounted and the other on foot, out-distanced the foot soldiers and escaped over the

Fort Baker - Old Mormon Fort, Las Vegas, Nevada.
Courtesy: The Author

mountains with several head of livestock. Tolles then made his way back to Camp Ruby.[23] (*See also* Camp on Silver Creek.)

On 3 June, Governor Blasdel, Lieutenant Colonel Charles McDermit, Lieutenant C.C. Warner, Surgeon A.F. Meachem and thirteen troopers of Company E, 1st Nevada Cavalry, arrived in Austin and met with local Indian leaders. Obtaining the Indians' pledge of peace, the civilians in the party went on to meet with other Indian groups. McDermit proceeded on toward Gravelly Ford with Seamonds and a portion of his command.[24]

Many well-preserved old buildings and the stark scenery of central Nevada make the trip interesting. Austin is located in Lander County on US 50 approximately 110 miles east of Fallon and 137 miles west of Ely. The historic buildings and main street provide a picturesque setting well worth the travel time.

Baker, Fort
Clark County

Originally established as a Mormon fort, it became well known as an important source of water and relief for travelers on the Old Spanish Trail. The site was documented by many early travelers including Captain John C. Fremont who, during his visit on 3 May 1844, described the water as a clear, narrow stream 4-5 feet deep, warm, but with good taste. In 1850, the Mormons built a fort 150 foot square with 10 foot high, two-foot thick adobe walls "in a grassy valley ½ mile wide and 2-3 miles long."[25] In 1857, the fort was abandoned when they were recalled to Salt Lake City in anticipation of a fight against General Johnson's Utah expedition. The site was used intermittently by military patrols and the Overland Mail.

During the Civil War, the post was designated 'Fort Baker' in honor of Colonel Edward Dickinson Baker, 71st Pennsylvania Volunteer Infantry, who was killed 21 October 1861, in the battle of Ball's Bluff, VA.[26] Although it was never actually used as anything more than a temporary camp, the Fort played an important role as part of a plan of deception. On 19 December 1861, Colonel James Henry Carelton, Commander of the 1st California Infantry, announced plans to re-establish the fort: "Have your company get in perfect readiness for important field service with the re-establishment of Fort Mojave and of Fort Baker at Las Vegas on the Salt Lake road. Have a drill at the target, three shots per man a day for ten days, commencing at 100 yards and increasing ten yards each day. Have also two hours' drill each day at skirmish drill. Make a tabular report of every shot to me. Be careful of your clothing; have it carefully mended, particularly the men's shoes."[27] The Confederate threat to the southwest was real and plans to recruit a force in southern California went on throughout most of the war. Also, the Confederate Cavalry was moving to take control of the New Mexico-Arizona Territory.Carelton's intent was to deceive the Confederates into believing there was a large military presence in the Las Vegas area.

Fort Baker was supposedly garrisoned with four companies of 1st California Volunteer Infantry to protect commerce between Los Angeles and Salt Lake City. To deceive the Confederate spies and sympathizers in California, goods on supply trains were prominently marked with Fort Baker and Fort Mojave as destinations. In actuality the supplies were sent to Fort Yuma for use by the California Column en route to fight the Confederate Texas Volunteers fighting in Arizona and New Mexico.[28] There is no indication in the official records that troops were actually stationed at Fort Baker during the Civil War or that the site was ever used by any military units other than as temporary quarters by transient military patrols.

Located at 908 North Las Vegas Boulevard in Las Vegas, the buildings have been reconstructed and are maintained today by the Nevada Division of State Parks as a historic site.[29]

Basse's Ferry
Humboldt County

Basse's Ferry was a crossing on the Humboldt River near the present-day town of Ragtown. During the summer campaign of 1864, Captain A.B. Wells crossed the Humboldt here with fifty men of Company D, 1st Nevada Cavalry, en route to Smoke Creek Station[30] From I-80 take exit 168 (10 miles west of Winnemucca). Travel north on the gravel road to the Humboldt River. The exact site is unknown, but is believed to be in this vicinity.

Battle Creek
Humboldt County

In spite of continuing pressure from the cavalry in 1865, Indian raids were becoming even more intense along the road between the Humboldt River settlements and Camp McDermit. Following their defeat at Leonard Creek, Black Rock Tom's surviving Paiute, Shoshone and Bannock followers gathered in an isolated area farther north in the Black Rock Range. In late December of 1865, they joined with the band of Captain John, a Warner Lake Shoshone Chief. Captain John was reported to have been the slayer of Lieutenant Colonel Charles McDermit in August of that year. As long as the killers were at large, the region was not safe for unescorted travel. Relentless in their efforts to find the killers, the 2nd California Cavalry maintained their pursuit.

On 8 January 1866, Captain G.D. Conrad departed from Dun Glen. Accompanying him were thirty-five soldiers of Company B, 2nd California Cavalry, nine civilian volunteers, and twelve friendly Paiute scouts led by Paiute Captain Soo (also known as Mo-guan-no-ga, *see* Williams Station). After camping at Willow Point Station on the night of the ninth they departed late in the evening on the tenth to avoid observation of their movement into Queen's (Quinn) River Valley. During the night they arrived at Cane Springs where they met Second Lieutenant Robert L. Duncan from Camp McDermit. Duncan brought an additional twenty-five soldiers from Company I, of the same regiment. A heavy snow fell during the night. The weather concealed their move and favored surprise in their planned attack, but made it a miserable time to be in the field. In the hope of spotting Indian camp fires, Conrad, Captain Thomas Ewing and Sergeant Louis Korble rode to the top of a nearby mountain overlooking the valley, but saw nothing. The main body left camp early on the morning of the eleventh. The bitter cold, fresh snow and muddy ground slowed their twenty-mile march to the Queen's River. The evening of the eleventh they crossed the river and camped for the night.

During the night Conrad, Ewing, civilian W.K. Parkinson with four soldiers and Indians Soo and Bob, made the seven-mile trip to the crest of the next mountain range to again scout for the Indian campfires. This time their efforts were rewarded. About twelve miles from the base of the hill they spotted numerous fires indicating a large camp in the east arm of the Black Rock Desert. They returned to Duncan's camp on the river and gave the order to be ready to move out at 11:30 p.m. that night. Equipment not needed for the fight was placed on the wagons and after eating, issuing extra ammunition, and preparing the horses, the column departed the 'Queen's River' camp precisely at 11:30 p.m. They had twenty more miserable miles to cover. Their march included crossing a large creek, riding through marshy stream banks and trying to stay in contact with each other in the dark—made worse by the steamy fog of several hot springs.

In part to avoid talking among the soldiers and in part to maintain control due to the rough terrain, mud, and snow, the soldiers moved single file in a long column. At 3:00 on the morning of the twelfth they arrived at their rally point. As close to the Indian camp as they dared be they halted to regroup. With nearly three hours to wait before the dawn light would permit an attack, the intense cold seriously threatened the success of the mission. Unprotected from the elements and weary from their ride, men and horses were literally freezing in the bitter cold.[31] To relieve both the tension and the pain of the cold Conrad made the unorthodox decision to have his already exhausted men dismount and run in circles for nearly the full three hours before daybreak. "Even with this extraordinary effort to save themselves, over 20 men were frozen—their hands, feet or faces. Notwithstanding all they suffered, not a murmur of complaint was uttered by the soldiers. The horses huddled up closer together, and were covered with a white mantle of frost; seeming frozen together."[32]

As the eastern horizon turned from black to a dark grey, Conrad had his soldiers make the final check of their equipment. Cinches tightened, horse shoes clinched, percussion caps put in place, canteens filled, loose equipment secured, the soldiers made ready. At daybreak, one by one, Indian fires began to appear. Following the classic doctrine of the time, Conrad divided the command into three columns for the attack. Duncan with Company I took the right flank; Sergeant Korble with men from Company B took the left flank; and Conrad advanced in the center with a composite of soldiers, civilians and Indian scouts. The soldiers remounted their horses. The two flanking elements, in column, moved about 1200-1300 yards on either side of the captain. They advanced simultaneously on the Indian camp. When they were within a mile of the camp they moved abreast of each other, advancing in one line.

The camp was on the eastern side of the Black Rock Range in a large basin about three and a half miles across. Terrain, cover and concealment favored the Indians' position. Tall grasses, cattails along the stream and sage brush provided excellent concealment. Numerous gullies and ravines broke up the land surface and gave good cover. A slight upward slope from the creek worked against the already tired cavalry horses and their riders. The battleground was ideal for small group fighting using bows and arrows and other close weapons. A frost and near fog reduced visibility to approximately one hundred yards.

The advancing cavalry was spotted when they were about a mile from their objective. With only two or three minutes to prepare for the battle, the Indians quickly clustered around natural defenses in small groups of four to six warriors. The cavalry quickened their pace. By keeping their interval and maneuvering with strict discipline in accordance with their plan, they were able to nearly encircle the Indians before shots were fired. From this position they began an advance toward the center of the camp. While the soldiers lacked the advantages provided to the Indians by the site, they had superior numbers and a discipline rooted in experience in similar battles. It was from Korble's side that the first shots were fired. The noise of the fight on the left provided enough distraction for the soldiers in the center and on the right to arrive nearly on top of the Indians before fighting began in their part of the circle. The Indians fought with great fury and courage born of the desperation of having no avenues of retreat. The battle lasted nearly two and a half hours. The determination, skill and valor of the Indians was noted in later reports. Though brave, their limited ammunition and bows and arrows were no match for the better armed and larger force of cavalry soldiers. Near the end, the fighting was reduced to two strong points of Indian resistance. From one of these Indian Captain John carried his fight to the end making no attempt at escape. He was eventually felled with a shot to the head fired by militia Captain Rapley. By John's body was a bow and a quiver of arrows, as well as the rifle he had used to slay McDermit.

Bravery was the common trait of both forces in this final contest between seasoned soldiers and warriors. Singled out for his courage was Doctor Snow, a civilian physician who had accompanied Duncan. He moved from soldier to soldier, checking wounds and providing an antidote for those hit by poisoned arrows. Although considerably older than the soldiers he attended, Doctor Snow had endured the hardships of the trail, as well as the bitter cold of the season to provide the medical attention needed in this type of combat.[33]

The cavalry's official report states, "Corporal Biswell and Private Allen of Company I, and Privates Thomas A. Duffield, John Riley, and Richard Shultz of Company B, 2nd California Cavalry, were wounded. Two horses were killed and nine wounded."[34] Duffield's wound, a rifle ball in the arm, was serious enough to result in his discharge for disability a few weeks later.[35] The other wounds were from arrows; Biswell in the head; Allen in the leg; Riley in the arm; and Shultz in the shoulder. One of Soo's Indians, Jim Dunne, received an arrow wound in the back. Both Duncan's and Korble's horses were among the severely wounded animals. Korble's horse survived the return trip as far as Paradise Valley and then died.[36]

Thirty-five Indian bodies were found on the battlefield. There were five to ten women in the group, two of which had been killed in the fighting. The others were given provisions and allowed to tend the dead and leave. With three inches of snow on the ground an easy search was made for tracks of escaping Indians. None were found. Later reports from Indians indicated an additional three braves had hidden in the vegetation, but died from their wounds. Other stories tell of an Indian survivor who, though shot in both legs, hid in the vegetation and then climbed over the mountains to the west after the battle.[37]

After publishing accounts of the battle the *Humboldt Register* came under criticism for citing the bravery of eighty men armed with Maynard rifles fighting thirty-five Indians mainly armed with bows and arrows. In response they published the following: "Certain facts need to be understood, to have the correct conception of the affair. The clouds of flying frost obliged the riflemen to come to close range, in order to see their enemy. This was in favor of the bow shots. The arrows were known, after the first one had been shot, to be poisoned. This was chilling information. Then, these wild Indians would stand up and deliberately fire their deadly missiles after receiving in their carcasses as many as six of those heavy conical shots which the Maynard carries; and would let fly their arrows with the last breath; whereas one of the leadon [sic] shots so carried by them would have knocked any white man out of time. Virtually, each Indian had about seven lives."[38]

The Leonard Creek entry (below) contains a detailed discussion of the geographic site names for the Battle Creek and Fish Creek-Leonard Creek battles. Directions to both sites are also given with the Leonard Creek entry. Both creeks are within a few miles of each other. Leonard Creek is on the east slope of the Pine Forest Range and Battle Creek is a few miles to the south on the east slope of the Black Rock Range.

Battle Lakes Camp Site (Humboldt Sinks)
Pershing County

During his 1829 crossing of the Great Basin, Peter Ogden followed the Humboldt River to its sinks west of present-day Lovelock. On the night of 19 May 1829, he encountered a group of Paiute Indians and, after offering them tobacco, he camped for the night. Near the same site in 1833-34, Joseph Walker also camped near "shallow ponds at the mouth of the Humboldt River." His encounter was less friendly. Theft of beaver traps set by his party led to a disagreement and ultimately a skirmish in which several Paiutes were killed. Walker's party left the area in haste to avoid further conflict. As a result, the site was recorded by Walker's scribe as the Battle Lakes Campsite.

The Humboldt Sinks are the brackish lakes in the playa/marsh area east of Exit 93 (Toulon) on I-80. The area is managed today by the U.S. Fish and Wildlife Service.

Battle Mountain Battle Site
Lander County

Two stories tell of the battle for which Battle Mountain is named. One is of a skirmish between a road-building party led by John Kirk and a Shoshone raiding party in 1857.[39] A second story relates how a wagon train captain named Pierson and twenty-two emigrants were attacked by Paiutes near where the Reese River drains into the Humboldt River, also in 1857.[40] Either story will do; however, the fact that both battles occurred in 1857 causes the student of history to wonder if Kirk and Pierson later drew straws to decide which incident would get credit. It is a safe bet that the mountain was named before the town. Battle Mountain is located on Interstate 80 approximately two-hundred miles east of Reno.

Beale's Crossing
Clark County

Named for Navy Lieutenant Edward Beale, this crossing on the Colorado River was used in 1857 as part of the camel experiment in the southwest deserts.[41] The crossing is located on the Colorado River near the southern tip of Nevada.

Benton, Fort
Mineral County

On his third western expedition, Captain John Fremont, U.S. Topographical Engineers, passed near here in 1845. He named his campsite for his father-in-law Senator Thomas Hart Benton. Although not verified, local custom identifies several rock ruins four miles northwest of Luning, Nevada, as the site of the 'fort.' From Luning go three miles north on US 95 to the junction of a dirt road on the west side of US 95. Travel west five miles to the rock ruins.[42]

Big Antelope Creek, Camp
Pershing County

A detachment of California Cavalry was temporarily stationed here during the Indian uprising in the spring of 1865. This was one of many private stations established to support mining and commerce in the area. Nothing remains at the site other than scattered metal fragments and a few aligned stones marking foundations and tent walls of the mining camp. From exit 145 (Imlay) on I-80 take the improved road to the west approximately fifteen miles to where it crosses the Antelope Range.[43]

Big Meadows
Pershing County

Big Meadows was the homeland for Paiute Chief Mo-guan-no-ga, called Captain Soo by the whites. The large grassy flat had been a traditional camp site and winter home of Paiute Indians for centuries. In May of 1860, it was Chief Mo-guan-no-ga who led the war party in the raid on Williams Station. He also fought in the defeat of Major William Ormsby in the first battle at Pyramid Lake. A strong advocate of war against the whites, he was an excellent horseman and a fierce warrior.[44]

By 1863 his attitude toward the whites changed. He came to realize that the Indians could win small skirmishes or successfully raid wagons and isolated stations, but in the long run his people would pay for the depredations and ultimately be defeated. Accepting that there was no way to drive the whites out of the country he began serving as a guide for the military. Whether motivated by a desire to eliminate rivals or to protect his own band he participated in some of the most violent fighting in the Nevada Indian Wars. A merciless victor he was as quick to kill defeated Paiutes as he was to kill whites in his earlier days.[45] He was eventually killed in a dispute with his cousin and brother over leadership of the band. (*See* Pyramid Lake.)

Soo and several of his followers assisted the California and Nevada Volunteers in locating and engaging various renegade bands, including the band led by Black Rock Tom.[46] Several days after the November 1865 battle at Leonard Creek, Black Rock Tom tried to surrender to Soo at Big Meadows. He went to Big Meadows where Soo then asked civilian authorities to take custody of Tom. On 18 December, First Lieutenant R.A. Osmer reported to Fort Churchill his receipt of a letter from Thomas Stark, "who informs me that Capt Tom and two of his tribe of Indians, the same that I had the fight with on the 17th of November, 1865, have come to his place and surrendered themselves to him and sued for peace, and want to form some treaty."[47]

On 21 December, soldiers from Company K, 2nd California Cavalry, took Tom into custody. Soo was quick to tell the soldiers that Tom would not honor his word and his peace gestures would not last. Although Tom apparently hoped to surrender and thus gain peace, civilians convinced him he would be hanged once he arrived at Fort Churchill. An entry in the returns of Company K tells what happened: "After four days march I arrived at Blake's Station, where the citizens turned over to me a notorious Indian called 'Black Rock Tom.' After being put in charge of the guard, he tried to escape, and was shot dead by some of the command."[48]

Big Meadows lays along Interstate 80 and the Humboldt River, extending upstream east from the present day town of Lovelock to the Humboldt Sinks. The area is now occupied by farm lands.

Black, Camp

Camp Black was a temporary military supply point used to support campaigns in northwestern Nevada during the summer of 1865. Captain Albert Hahn, commander of Company I, 6th California Infantry, is credited with naming this supply point after Colonel Henry Moore Black.[49] The exact site of the camp is unknown and may have only been a reference to the frequently relocated field trains as they followed the movement of the combat soldiers they supported. Camp Black is reported to have been twenty-five miles northwest of Summit Lake near Massacre Lake. Another report gives the location in Paradise Valley.[50] It is doubtful that the trains remained stationary for more than a few days or weeks at a time. (*See also* Camps Overend, Pollock, Zabrieskie.)

Black Rock Desert
Pershing and Humboldt Counties

The Black Rock Desert is a vast playa devoid of all vegetation and subject to periodic inundation by winter and spring runoff from adjacent mountains. The major water source is the Quinn (also Queen's) River. From Gerlach, Nevada, the desert runs forty to fifty miles to the northeast with two arms extending to the north separated by the Black Rock Range. Captain John Fremont reported this wasteland on 2 January 1844. The Applegate-Lassen Trail crosses the desert near the center of its southern edge and continues north along the western arm to High Rock Canyon. The Black Rock Desert was ringed by some of the most significant fighting of the Indian War in Nevada. Several campaigns skirted the edges or crossed the Black Rock Desert in pursuit of renegade bands.

If you are visiting the area make local inquiry before driving out on the playa surface. If it appears wet, do not drive on the playa. The area is predominately public land and recently received special status through Congressional designation as a National Conservation Area under management by the Bureau of Land Management. In addition to the sites identified in this book, it is a good place to observe natural geologic formations, native flora and fauna, and wild horses common to the Great Basin. The Black Rock Desert is the site of various recreational, scientific and cultural events such as setting the world land speed record and the Burning Man Festival held annually on Labor Day weekend.

Black Slate Mountains
Humboldt County

On 11 February 1867, Second Lieutenant John Lafferty and Sergeant John Kelley left Camp Scott with a detachment of thirteen soldiers from Company A, 8th U.S. Cavalry. With six days' rations, their mission was to scout for Indians in the vicinity of Eden Valley and further to the southeast. After camping on the

Little Humboldt River at the mouth of Eden Valley, they proceeded south toward the Humboldt River. Two additional days of scouting produced no results. On the fifteenth, when enroute back toward Camp Scott, they encountered fifteen Indians encamped in the foothills of Black Slate Mountain. Dividing his small command, he moved to encircle the group. Sergeant Kelley, with five soldiers, was sent to cover the Indians' most likely avenue of escape, but the battle began before he was in position. Five Indians were killed and the remainder escaped. The cavalry suffered no losses. Lafferty's report states:

> The camp was situated at the head of a small ravine and at least six miles from the nearest water. They had two large camp kettles, and were in the act of melting snow. They seemed to be well provided with food for the winter, and had a large quantity of grass seeds. We also found several fish and rabbit nets, a hatchet, and several knives, and many other articles belonging to the whites. There were also two rifles and a pistol in the party; one fired his rifle, but missed his aim, and then succeeded in making good his escape. The other attempted fire, but his gun missed, when he received a bullet through the head, killing him instantly. I kept up the pursuit until sundown, when after destroying everything of value we could find, except the rifle and pistol and some nets, which we brought into camp, we mounted and proceeded direct to the river, a distance of fifteen miles, arriving at 11 o'clock at night and encamped.[51]

Black Slate Mountain is most likely the feature known today as Golconda Butte. It is slightly over eight miles north-northwest of the Golconda exit (Exit 194) on Interstate 80 east of Winnemucca. (*See also* Camp Scott for additional information on Lafferty and Kelley.)

Buckland Station
Lyon County

Built in September 1857 by Samuel Sanford Buckland, this station served emigrants and commerce along the Carson Branch of the California Emigrant Trail. From the east it was the first major station after the Overland Trail merged with a branch of the

California Trail. In 1860 Buckland invested in the Pony Express and expanded his station to support this venture.[52] On 11 May 1860, militia Major William M. Ormsby camped here with his force of volunteers en route to their ill-fated battle at Pyramid Lake. Following a night of revelry and self assurance, the group was organized into four squads here and departed for the Truckee River and Pyramid Lake to the north. Four days after their departure survivors began straggling back with news of their disastrous losses. Word was funneled back to Virginia and Carson Cities where preparations began immediately for an expected all-out attack by the victorious Indians. The attack never came and within a few weeks regular U.S. Army soldiers and a much better organized militia force rallied here for a second battle near Pyramid Lake. A few months later construction began on Fort Churchill a short distance to the west and Buckland Station became a source of produce, civilian goods, whiskey, and gambling for soldiers from the post.[53] When Fort Churchill was abandoned the post and its buildings were sold at auction and much of the lumber was used by or marketed through Buckland's business enterprise. The site is now owned by the Nevada Division of State Parks and is located on US 95, nine miles south of Silver Springs, Nevada.

Buffalo Slough/Buffalo Springs
Washoe County

This station was used as a watering stop and occasional camp site on the Noble's Cutoff, later called the Chico-Boise Road and the Honey Lake-Humboldt River Road. It is mentioned in several military reports as a rest stop between the Camp at Smoke Creek Station and Deep Hole. On 7 July 1864, it served as a stop for a thirty-man detachment from Company D, 1st Nevada Cavalry, under First Lieutenant John Littlefield. During the uprising in the spring of 1865, it was used frequently by soldiers patrolling the commerce routes through the area.

It is located on the northern edge of the Smoke Creek Desert between Deep Hole and Smoke Creek Station. From Gerlach, Nevada go nine miles north on State Highway 447 to the Washoe

County Road on the west side of the highway. Then travel west sixteen and one half miles on the improved gravel road. Nothing remains of the station that was located a short distance up the Buffalo Slough drainage.

Butte Station
White Pine County

Butte Station served both the Overland Stage and the Pony Express. On 15 May 1859 Captain James Hervey Simpson, U.S. Topographical Engineers, camped near here and gave one of the better accounts of George Chorpenning's early east-west mail enterprise. "The mail during the winter was carried on a pack mule, which was sometimes led and sometimes driven. The rate of travel (which was accomplished) was 60 miles every twenty four hours, changing every 20-30 miles ... ."[54] A year later, the Pony Express was carrying the mail at a much faster rate. The station was burned on 27 June, during the Indian uprising in 1860. Although a minor station and a poor source of water, it was rebuilt. In October 1860, overland traveler Sir Richard Burton reported that the station master, "built us a roaring fire, added meat to our supper of coffee and doughboy, and cleared by a summary process amongst the snorers, places on the floor of Robber's Roost or Thieves' Delight, as the place is facetiously known throughout the countryside."[55]

Water at the original site was supplied by a hand-dug well that Simpson describes as, "barely sufficient for culinary purposes ... ." He continued, "Subsequent to this date in the summer, this point had to be abandoned by the mail company as a station on account of the well drying up. I have learned, however, that they have since found water in the vicinity, probably about two miles to the southeast where a Sho-sho-nee told us there was water."[56]

In all likelihood the station occupied more than one site within the pass in the northern end of the Butte Mountains. Only unmaintained ranch roads are found in this remote area today. Its approximate longitude and latitude are 115 degrees, 12 minutes north and 38 degrees and 56 minutes west. The projected legal description is approximately in the NW1/4 of Section 27, T. 24 N., R. 60. E. The entire area is public land.

California Emigrant Trail
Elko, Eureka, Lander, Humboldt, Pershing, Churchill, Lyon, Carson and Douglas Counties.

Following discovery of gold in California this was the major migration route for the pioneers across Nevada. The trail essentially follows the Humboldt River to the sinks near Lovelock. From there it crosses the most dreaded stretch through the Forty Mile Desert to the Carson River at Ragtown. Several mountain passes were used to cross the Sierra Nevada's into California. The Emigrant Trail remained a major route for east-west commerce and eventually became the route for the transcontinental railroad. Today the trail runs parallel to Interstate 80. Several events of the Indian War occurred at sites along the trail and are discussed in this text. From east to west they are: Humboldt Wells, Gravelly Ford, Camp Lyon, Big Meadows, Battle Lakes, Forty Mile Desert, Ragtown, Miller's Station, Dayton, Carson City, Genoa, and Friday's Station.

Call (Callville), Camp
Clark County

This Colorado River landing was established by and named for Mormon Bishop Anson W. Call in 1864. At that time the area was part of Pah Ute County in Arizona Territory. Congressional changes to Nevada's boundary added this region to the state in 1866. The townsite was later purchased with the intent of establishing a transfer point for commercial goods from steamships to wagons for trade between Salt Lake City and southern California. The first shipment of goods arrived on the steamship *Esmeralda* on 27 October 1866. A combination of unreliable river flows, development of irrigated agriculture in California and unwilling customers for California products in Utah eliminated the vision. Through some intense political maneuvering and exaggerated claims of Indian problems, Major General Irvin McDowell, Commander of the Department of the Pacific, agreed to establish Camp El Dorado on the Colorado River downstream from Callville. 'Fort' Call and Las Vegas were to be used as outliers from Camp El Dorado.

On 25 January 1867 one sergeant, nine privates and five others (wagoneers and teamsters) left Camp El Dorado for Callville. They took thirty days' supplies to establish Camp Call. The intent was to house a garrison of seven or eight soldiers and a paid civilian guide. The camp peaked at eighteen soldiers under command of the sergeant. The garrison had no mission or real purpose. On 9 May 1868, the order was issued to discontinue the outpost at Callville.[57]

The site can be approached by traveling thirty miles east from Henderson, Nevada, on State Highway 41. Today the site is presently under the waters of Lake Mead on the east side of the road between Boulder and Black Canyons on the Colorado River.[58] The land is administered by the National Park Service as part of Lake Mead National Recreation Area.

Camp Station
(*See* Grubbs Well)

Cane Springs
Humboldt County

Cane Springs was a reliable source of water and forage on the north-south route from the Humboldt River to destinations in Idaho. Following the Indian raids in Paradise Valley in the spring of 1865, local citizens armed themselves and went in search of any bands of warriors they could find. On 15 April, the civilians surprised an Indian party at Cane Springs. They charged the Indian camp and at the end of the fight they "brought away with them eighteen scalps as trophies of their work."[59] The action and the choice of words used to describe it was indicative of the intense feeling of the time and the nature of the hostilities in early 1865. This was but one of many incidents in a cycle of attacks and reprisals perpetuated by both the whites and the Indians.

Cane Springs was a convenient rally point between the camp at Dun Glen and Camp McDermit. Prior to the battle on 12

January 1866 at Battle Creek, Captain G.D. Conrad, Indian Captain Soo and soldiers of Company B, 2nd California Cavalry, from Dun Glen met here with Second Lieutenant Robert L. Duncan with additional soldiers from Company I, of the same regiment from Fort McDermit. From here they continued their journey to the west in pursuit of Indian Captain John, the Warner Lake Shoshone who had killed Lieutenant Colonel Charles McDermit five months earlier.[60] (*See* Battle Creek.)

Take US 95 north from Winnemucca thirty miles to State Route 140. Travel west about two miles west (toward DeNio) on State Route 140. Cane Springs is about one mile south of State Route 140 on private land.

Cape Horn Station
Lander County

The name of this station is a rare glimpse at the thoughts and the subtle humor on the minds of Nevada's early pioneers. The main competition for the overland mail contractors were the ships that made the sea voyage around Cape Horn at the southern tip of the South American continent. In the early 1850s, 'Around the Horn' took about thirty days for delivery with no guarantees of either arrival or frequency. By comparison, George Chorpenning's mail in 1851 took fifty-three days using a land route across Nevada along the Humboldt River. The service was subject to the whims of nature's elements and unpredictable Indian attacks. Following the murder of his partner, Absalom Woodward, and four others in November 1851, Chorpenning's crew deserted his enterprise and he eventually lost his first contract in 1852.

By 1855, the ocean route included a land leg by rail across the Isthmus of Panama. Delivery only took twenty-two days from the east coast to California. Mail was delivered reliably on a semi-monthly basis.[61] On 1 July 1858, Chorpenning was awarded another contract for $130,000, nearly ten times the amount of his 1851 contract. The 1858 contract followed what is now known as the Overland Trail and incorporated the Cape Horn Station. His mail service lasted until May 1860 at which time it failed for financial reasons. It was replaced by the Pony Express.

The Cape Horn Station is approximately one mile north of US 50 and eight miles west of the Bureau of Land Management Hickison Petroglyph Recreation Area.

Carlin Military Reservation
Elko County

Once the transcontinental railroad was completed and fully in service, the decision was made to relocate the troops from Fort Halleck to a more convenient site. A 960-acre tract was selected on Maggie Creek one and a half miles north of present day Carlin, Nevada. It was to be designated Fort Carlin. An Executive Order, signed 9 March 1874, segregated the land, and more detailed planning began. On 7 April 1875, the Executive Order was amended, changing the land description. By then, Indian troubles in northern Nevada were nearly nonexistent. The post was never constructed and the land reverted to the U.S. Department of the Interior on 20 March 1886.[62]

Carson City

The townsite was originally the headquarters for the Eagle Ranch established in 1851. In 1857, land for a town was purchased from the Ranch. In 1858, Major William Ormsby acquired the land and laid out the townsite. In 1859, Captain James H. Simpson, U.S. Topographical Engineers, described it as having a dozen buildings and two stores. The following year, Bolivar Roberts, the Pony Express Division Agent charged with overseeing operations from Dry Creek Station west to California, established a station using a building on Carson Street between 4th and 5th Streets.[63] In May 1860, following the defeat of Ormsby at Pyramid Lake, 'Camp Carson' was established in the Penrod Hotel.[64]

Nevada was separated from Utah on 3 March 1861, and was officially designated a Territory.[65] Within a few weeks, the Civil War began. As regular U.S. Army units were sent to the east, locally recruited volunteer units took their place. No quota was assigned to Nevada. However, Captain Charles D. Douglas from California arrived to recruit for the newly authorized 2nd California Infantry. Responding to the promise of fighting 'Johnny Reb,' several citizens quickly enlisted. By October 1860, fifty-nine volunteers had been obtained to serve in Company F, 2nd California Infantry. Rather than moving to the east as had been anticipated, the new volunteers were marched off to the west for Indian fighting in Northern California. In all, one hundred and fifty-nine volunteers were recruited for service in the 2nd and 3rd California Infantry as well as the 2nd California Cavalry.[66]

The patriotic fever was epidemic. Other than the militia there was no full time military presence in the capital. A request was made to the Army in San Francisco for a company to be assigned to Carson City. In response, Captain George F. Price, commanding Company M, 2nd California Cavalry, was ordered to Carson City in May 1862. On 13 June 1862, he established a temporary camp about five miles north of Carson City on the south shore of Washoe Lake. (*See* Camp Nye.) After some reconnaissance he reported back to San Francisco that Indians in the vicinity of Carson City, as well as Aurora were all peaceful.[67] The company was subsequently reassigned.

When Nevada become a State on 31 October 1863, Carson City remained the capital. All was quiet there until rumors of a Confederate takeover became so frequent that an actual uprising was anticipated. On 7 September 1864, two officers and fifty enlisted soldiers of Company C, 1st Nevada Cavalry, were ordered to the area from Fort Churchill.[68] Within a month, Major Milo George of the 1st Nevada Cavalry was ordered to establish a post for two companies.[69] Shortly a new camp was established (*again see* Camp Nye) and Companies D and E, 1st Nevada Cavalry, moved from Fort Churchill to a post on the west side of the city.

Carson Sink Station
Churchill County

The Pony Express Company originally constructed the compound for the Carson Sink Station in March 1860. Bolivar Roberts and J.G. Kelly supervised the work. In May 1860, after word of the troubles at Pyramid Lake reached the area, about fifteen settlers assembled at the station for protection. Within a few days fifty Paiute warriors arrived. A few long-range shots were initially exchanged. The adobe walls and the size of the white force appeared to be more than the Indians wanted to handle. Neither side inflicted casualties and the Indians went in search of an easier target. By October 1860, the station included at least one frame building, an adobe corral, and exterior walls of a compound.[70]

In October 1863, a Walker Lake Paiute Chief, E-zed-wa, was killed along the Carson River near Fort Churchill. He had been en route to Virginia City to meet with rancher N.H.A. Mason to file a complaint regarding his overseer. The overseer, John F. Hale, met E-zed-wa on the trail and, learning of the chief's purpose, Hale plied the chief with liquor. Once he was drunk Hale killed him and dumped his body in the Carson River. In an attempt to cover up the crime, Hale also killed his horse. The chief's corpse was soon found and evidence clearly revealed the facts. The Indians were outraged by the murder. In response, Indian Captain George gathered about thirteen hundred Paiutes at Carson Sink.[71] Once assembled, they sent a message to Fort Churchill demanding justice for the death of the E-zed-wa. First Lieutenant Oscar Jewett, Company D, 1st Nevada Cavalry, was sent to meet with them. After much discussion the Indians accepted Jewett's settlement. The Indians returned to their homes in exchange for a wagon load of provisions, some clothing and $1000 in cash to be provided by Mason.[72]

The area referred to as Carson Sink in the 1860s is shown as Carson Lake on today's maps. Its southern edge, where the station was located, is approximately thirteen miles south of Fallon on US 95. Today nothing remains other than the melted outline of adobe walls. The sand dunes on the south side of the area are beginning to cover a portion of the site.[73]

Cherry Creek
White Pine County

The Cherry Creek Range contains several streams, an ample

supply of pine nuts, game animals and other natural resources used to support the hunting and gathering lifestyle common to many of the Indian tribes in Northern Nevada. Goshute Creek and other streams contain excellent fish habitat. Other than the stations along the Overland Trail, the region was uninhabited by the whites in the 1860s. It served as a natural retreat for Indians following their raids on remote stations, prospectors, and settlers in nearby valleys. When trouble between the Goshutes and whites along the Nevada-Utah border occurred in 1863, the Cherry Creek Range was one of the areas targeted by the soldiers. In August 1863, Lieutenant Josiah Hosmer, with soldiers from Company E, Third California Infantry, engaged a party of Goshutes in the Steptoe Valley about twenty miles north of the station at Cherry Creek. Five of the Indians were killed, with no reported losses to Hosmer's force.[74] (*See also* Egan Station, Duck Creek *and* Spring Valley.)

The Cherry Creek Range can be seen to the west along US 93 from Schellbourne north for approximately fifty miles. Most of the area is public land. The range is a fairly unintruded area even today and well worth the visit. Inquiry at the BLM Office in Ely, Nevada would be advisable before traveling in the area.

Churchill Barracks
(*See* Fort Churchill.)

Churchill, Fort
Lyon County
The queen of historic Nevada military posts, Fort Churchill, was established by Captain Joseph Stewart, 3rd U.S. Artillery, on 20 July 1860. This was shortly after the two battles with Indians near Pyramid Lake. The post was named in honor of Colonel Sylvester Churchill, Inspector General of the U.S. Army.[75] It was originally manned by Companies H, I & M, 3rd U.S. Artillery; Companies A & H, 6th U.S. Infantry; and detachments of Companies A & F, 1st U.S. Dragoons. Planned for a garrison of a thousand soldiers, it never housed more than eight hundred and averaged around three hundred. The post suffered from a variety

Fort Churchill, Nevada
Courtesy: Nevada Historical Society

of problems beginning with acute water pollution. The intended source, the Carson River, was found to be unsuitable due to contamination from upstream mining operations. This condition continued throughout the life of the post and is even a problem today. Shortly after the beginning of the Civil War, troops were reassigned to the east. The last U.S. Army commander was Major George A.H. Blake, 1st U.S. Dragoons. On 17 September 1861, he and the unit were reassigned to the east and federalized volunteer units from California assumed control. By November 1861, Major Charles McDermit, with two hundred soldiers of the 2nd California Cavalry, assumed command. Colonel Patrick Edward Connor, commanding the 3rd California Infantry, used the post briefly en route to Utah for Indian fighting in the northwestern Great Plains.

In 1863, Nevada was authorized one cavalry and one infantry battalion. Under McDermit's leadership officers were recruited from communities in the area and trained at Fort Churchill. The newly commissioned captains then recruited soldiers for their respective companies from the nearby communities. Initially, Companies A, B and C, 1st Nevada Cavalry were formed in this manner. After training at Fort Churchill they were given missions in a variety of locations. Other companies of the 1st Nevada Cavalry and 1st Nevada Infantry were thus trained. During their service all saw extensive duty fighting Indians throughout northern Nevada and the contiguous states, as well as Colorado and Wyoming.

On 13 August 1865, Lieutenant Colonel Ambrose E. Hooker, 6th California Infantry, took command of Fort Churchill following the death of Lieutenant Colonel McDermit.[76] (*See* Quinn River Camp Number 33.) Various units of the 2nd California Cavalry, 6th California Infantry, 1st Nevada Cavalry and 1st Nevada Infantry manned the post during the Civil War. The fort remained the hub of military activities in Nevada throughout the Civil War period and into late 1866, when command shifted to posts closer to hostilities at that time.

The 1st Nevada Infantry mustered out of federal service 23 December 1865. On 21 July 1866, the 1st Nevada Cavalry also mustered out along with several California volunteer units. They were replaced by regular U.S. Army units returning from the Civil War. The post was ordered abandoned as a fort on 19 May 1868, and ordered closed 29 September 1869, by Major General George H. Thomas.[77] In 1871, the site was relinquished to the General Land Office and sold at auction.

Epilogue: After mustering out, many Nevada and California volunteer officers and soldiers from Fort Churchill joined U.S. Army units. Several continued the military as a career until death or retirement. Ambrose Hooker took a commission as first lieutenant in the 8th U.S. Cavalry. He was promoted to captain in the all-black 9th U.S. Cavalry in March 1867, and remained in the service until his death in 1883.[78] Another notable example was Almond Brown Wells. From his beginnings as a twenty-two year old volunteer at Fort Churchill, he was the first individual to be certified and commissioned as second lieutenant through training at the Fort. After mustering out of the 1st Nevada Cavalry as a captain in 1866, he was accepted as a second lieutenant in the 8th U.S. Cavalry. He eventually served in the 1st, 4th, 8th, and 9th U.S. Cavalry regiments and through the years rose to the rank of colonel. He commanded the prestigious 1st U.S. Cavalry Regiment in 1901, a tribute to the man and to the foundation laid at Fort Churchill and through service in his learning years in northern Nevada.[79] Several others are covered elsewhere in this text.

Fort Churchill is located eight miles south of Silver Springs just west of on US Alt 95. The site is administered by the Nevada Division of State Parks. The ruins have been stabilized and visitors can walk about the grounds of the fort. The visitor's center and museum have very informative displays including interpretive materials, equipment of the time and a model of the post as it appeared at its peak. This is an excellent place to begin a visit to other military sites in Nevada. Plan also to visit nearby Buckland Station during your trip.

Clover Valley
(*See* Tuscarora Range.)

Cold Springs Station
Churchill County

Cold Springs Station and the area to the east were the locale for much of the Indian activity during the troubled summer of 1860. One of the few Pony Express riders killed by Indians rode into this station. He died of wounds received in an ambush along Edwards Creek to the east. After the fallen rider was cared for, the station manager, Jay G. Kelly, carried the mail over the trail for the next few days. Terrain dictated passage through the Edwards Creek drainage. Aspen groves provided excellent cover and a fertile opportunity for ambush. Within the week Kelly encountered Indians along the route and only luck and the speed of his horse got him through. Shortly after Kelly's encounter, two well-armed soldiers traveling the route were killed in another ambush and stripped of their clothes by Indians in the Edwards Creek Canyon. After killing the soldiers, the Indians moved on to Cold Springs Station. There they attacked the station, killed John Williams, the station keeper, and drove off the horses. Kelly was at Smith Creek Station at the time and escaped death. The following morning the Indians attacked Smith Creek Station. But this time, the express men successfully defended themselves within the rock walls of the station house.

Initially volunteers and settlers seeking refuge provided a level of protection for the stations. Concurrently western Pony Express manager William W. Finney requested seventy-five soldiers to be stationed along the route. When his request was denied he appealed to merchants in Sacramento. He was able to raise nearly $1500, which he used to hire civilian guards.[80] These were assigned to the most threatened stations. Defensive structures were added and existing facilities were reconfigured for siege. The Cold Springs Station became one of the most fortified stations along the Nevada portion of the route. The compound had walls seven feet high and two feet thick with gun ports and firing positions strategically placed for defense. When the Pony Express went out of business the facility was taken over by the Overland Stage company. Eventually a small detachment of soldiers was stationed here.[81]

To get there, go fifty-nine miles east of Fallon on US 50. The site is on public land on the north side of the road. Several rock ruins are found in the area. Nevada Historical Marker 83 marks the location of the Overland Mail Station (inside the chain link fence). About one-quarter mile east, a BLM interpretive display gives information about the Pony Express Station (two miles off the road to the southeast). The site is well worth the visit.

Como
Lyon County

A 'battle' at Como typified the trials and tribulations of many small-town militia units. On 13 October 1863, Paiute Chief Old Winnemucca met with the community leaders of Como to protest the further destruction of pinyon trees in the mountains adjacent to the town. He explained that the pine nuts were a major source of food for his people and that the "pine nut groves were the Indians' orchards." He explained that the Como residents were welcome to the fallen and dead timber, but were to leave the living trees alone. This warning was not heeded and in a few days sightings of Indians increased. They had come to harvest the nuts for the coming winter. Unaware of the Indians' peaceful purpose, residents of the small town became concerned and tensions elevated. Convinced that they were under siege by Indians, the local citizens called for assistance from the Army to relieve their plight. Twenty soldiers were sent to the town where they found no such siege. Not convinced that the Army's assessment of the situation was accurate, the Home Guard placed the town under martial law. A curfew was imposed, complete with password and countersign for use by Home Guard members. In the dark of night two militiamen, having forgotten the password, opened up on each other with pistols in a raging, but meaningless battle. In his haste to man his position, the town butcher tripped over his shot gun, discharging it, thus adding to the confusion. The tensions of 'battle' ended when daylight restored the calm. Only then were any Indians observed and they had only come to town to satisfy their curiosity regarding the shooting and noise of the previous night.[82]

Travel south from Dayton across the Carson River. Take the only road that leads into the Pine Nut Range for approximately nine and one half miles. The old Como townsite is on both sides of the road once you have passed through the saddle marking the ridge line of the Pine Nut Range.

Cottonwood Creek
Humboldt County

On 5 April 1865, Christopher Fearbourne and a Mr. Collins were killed by Indians at a cabin near Cottonwood Creek. At the beginning of the hostilities one of the white party, a Mr. Barber, rode for help. Upon his return with two others, they met an overwhelming Indian force. Unable to assist and badly outnumbered, Barber's group was forced to flee for their own safety. Upon reaching Willow Point the next morning they encountered First Lieutenant Joseph Wolverton with twenty-five men of Company D, 1st Nevada Cavalry. Wolverton immediately made the twenty-three mile ride back to Cottonwood Creek where he found the Indian's trail. The Indian horses were no match for the better bred and better nourished cavalry horses.[83] Approximately twelve miles from the creek he found the Indian party and killed ten in the battle that followed. Continuing the pursuit he killed two more near Martin Creek Gap. His only loss was one horse.[84] Wolverton returned to the burned out ranch on Cottonwood Creek, buried Fearbourne and Collins and resumed his pursuit toward Gravelly Ford.[85] (*See also* Paradise Valley *and* Camp 16). Within the month nearly every ranch from Fish Creek (to the northwest) to Dun Glen had been attacked.

On 23 April 1865, a peace agreement was reached between Paiute Chiefs Captain John and Captain Soo and militia Captains A.P.K. Safford, W.R. Usher, M.S. Bonnifield, and W.K. Parkinson. The Indians agreed to move all peaceful Paiutes out of the Humboldt River drainage and relocate them into the Carson River drainage. Any Indians remaining in the Humboldt drainage after one week would be considered hostile and killed on sight.[86] This agreement was made without the knowledge or consent of

Lieutenant Colonel McDermit. The agreement was also made with no funding or means to carry it out.[87] As a result many otherwise peaceful Indians remained in the area. Consequently many were killed without warning or provocation. Fighting became far more intense as one side's attack became the other side's justification for reprisal. Many Indians who had been ambivalent or peaceful before took up the fight against the whites. New coalitions formed among Indians who had previously been enemies.[88] The direct damage to both Indians and whites that followed this seemingly well-intended, but poorly planned, agreement can only be imagined.

Cottonwood Creek is one of the larger streams flowing to the southeast from the Santa Rosa Mountains. It runs through the village of Paradise Valley. The site of the initial Indian attack is near the toe of the east slope of the range. (*See also* Camp Scott). Martin Creek flows to the east of Paradise Valley. It is believed that the site of Wolverton's second encounter was in the uppermost reaches of Martin Creek near the crest of the mountains.

Cottonwood Canyon
Elko County

Carrying out orders given to him at Camp 16, First Lieutenant William G. Seamonds, with soldiers from Company B, 1st Nevada Infantry, scouted the area southeast of Gravelly Ford through late July 1865. After resupply at Camp Ruby on 25 July, he resumed scouting from the Humboldt River to the north with an Indian guide and fifteen of his infantry soldiers on horseback. In Cottonwood Canyon north of Humboldt Wells (today Wells, Nevada) they came upon Chief Zelanwick. In the fight that followed on 31 July 1865, the chief and eleven of his Indian warriors were killed. Sergeant Edwin D. Sherrill was wounded by a barbed arrow in the neck. He apparently survived his wounds, for many years later he applied for a military pension from his home in Pennsylvania.[89] Which Cottonwood Canyon or Cottonwood Creek was involved in the fight is unknown. In general, the site is northeast of Gravelly Ford and north of Wells.

Cottonwood Station
(*See* Truckee River Bend.)

Cottonwood Island
Clark County

Cottonwood Island was in the Colorado River about twenty-five miles downstream from Camp El Dorado. There being no forage available to feed livestock, seven or eight soldiers from Company D, 9th U.S. Infantry, were sent to the island to tend twenty head of cattle. The livestock were intended to supply fresh beef for the soldiers at Camp El Dorado. Spring run off flooded the island and drowned or drove the cattle from the island. Soldiers continued to be rotated through duty on Cottonwood Island on the pretext of searching for the missing cattle. Following a board of survey regarding the missing cattle, the last soldiers were removed from the island on 24 November 1867.[90] Cottonwood Island was an ephemeral island that has long since been washed away by the water of the Colorado River. Its general location was in the vicinity of the upper reaches of Lake Havasu.

Dayton
Lyon County

Dayton was one of the original Pony Express stations and also served the Overland Mail.[91] It was home for the Dayton Guards, a militia artillery unit.[92] On 9 August 1864 soldiers from Fort Churchill were sent to the town to restore order following a lynching. Troops from Company F, 1st Nevada Cavalry, under the command of Major Milo George accompanied Governor Nye as he read "the Riot Act" from the Court House. Order was restored and there were no more lynchings (at least until the next one).[93]

Deep Hole, Camp
Washoe County

Because of the good water and abundant forage, Deep Hole was frequently used by soldiers throughout the Indian campaigns in the Black Rock-Smoke Creek Desert area. It was a reliable source of water on the road between Honey Lake, California, and trails to Idaho and central Nevada. On 27-28 July 1864, Lieutenant John Littlefield and thirty soldiers from Company D, 1st Nevada Cavalry, camped here and reported, "... arrived at Deep Hole at 4 p.m.; distance of thirty four miles [from Smoke Creek Station]. Found water and hay for horses. During the night three men deserted, taking with them three Government horses, three saddles and bridles, three revolvers, and two carbines. July 28 left Deep Hole 6 a.m.; arrived [Trego] Hot Springs 4.30 p.m.; ..."[94] Littlefield was en route from Honey Lake, California, to Unionville, Nevada, to investigate rumors of a pending takeover of the town by Confederate sympathizers. The site was named for the local mining district and served briefly as a Post Office until 1867.[95]

The year 1864 was quiet. In the spring of 1865 the area again became unsafe. In a report on 10 July 1865, Captain W.L. Knight reported from Smoke Creek, "The detachment of Nevada Cavalry stationed at Deep Hole, thirty miles from here, is camped here tonight on its way back to Churchill. The man living at Deep Hole came with them, and thinks the Indians will make a raid on him as soon as they learn the detachment is gone. The sergeant in charge of the detachment reported to me that he saw Indian sign near the station the day before he left."[96] Patrols from Knight's company maintained order by patrolling in the Deep Hole area from the Smoke Creek Station.

Deep Hole is located in the northern end of the Smoke Creek Desert. Go north from Gerlach nine miles on State Route 81. Turn west on the maintained gravel road approximately two and one half miles. Location of the military campsites varied around the wet meadow to the south. This site is on private land.

Desert Wells Camp
Lyon County

This was an Overland Stage station approximately thirteen miles east of Dayton. Another 'Desert Wells Camp' is also on Herbert Hart's list of forts and is reported as having been fifteen miles north of Fallon. Nothing is known of military use, if any, at

Diamond Springs Station Marker
Courtesy: The Author

the site. Like many of the stations along the Overland Trail, there probably were transient units passing through the station in the early 1860s.

Diamond Springs Station
Lander County

Diamond Springs Station was used heavily by travelers and soldiers en route between California and Salt Lake City. The site served the Overland Stage and the Pony Express, as well as serving as a telegraph station. Colonel Patrick Edward Connor camped here in 1862 with elements of the 3rd California Volunteer Infantry during their march to Camp Douglas, Utah. The valley, mountain range, and springs are named either for the diamond-like gem stones found in the area or for prospector Jack Diamond who lived at the springs before the Pony Express.[97]

From the north edge of Eureka, Nevada take Lander County Road 101 north approximately twenty-nine miles to a ranch complex on the west side of the road. A monument on the east side of the road commemorates the site. An alternate account identifies rock ruins in a cottonwood grove a short distance farther north as the site. Most likely, remnants of the Pony Express station are incorporated into the ranch facilities. This site is on private land.

Disaster Peak
Humboldt County

In May 1864, a party of seven miners was attacked by a group of Indians near this site. Four of the miners, including G.W. Dodge, were killed by the Indians. One of the three survivors, a Mr. Noble, held off the Indians while the remaining two gathered their horses. Noble was wounded in the neck, shoulder and groin. Once the horses were gathered, the three men quickly mounted and escaped to Star City to report the incident. On 4 June 1864, the *Humboldt Register* reported that Captain Thomas Ewing, with soldiers from Company B, 2nd California Volunteer Cavalry, returned to the area and killed two Bannocks, one of whom was wearing a shirt belonging to "one of the four men killed ... ."[98]

Take US 95 north from Winnemucca thirty-one miles to State Route 140. Travel west on State Route 140 (toward DeNio) slightly over fourteen miles to the Kings River Road. Turn north, cross the Quinn River and continue up the Kings River Valley. At approximately thirty-four miles take the gravel road to the northeast. Disaster Peak is the taller of the two peaks to the north of the road. Take the gravel road approximately five miles up China Creek. Unimproved roads can get you closer to the base, but this is not recommended.

Donna Schee Springs
Humboldt County

Donna Schee Springs was a temporary camp site frequently used on expeditions from Dun Glen and Saint Mary's Crossing into the remote region between Paradise Valley and the east arm of the Black Rock Desert. In his report following the 17 November 1865 battle at Leonard Creek (called Fish Creek at the time) First Lieutenant R.A. Osmer stated that his command "... marched to Dunshea [sic] Springs - distance 35 miles ... ."[99] In a military context, Donna Schee Springs was merely another campsite on one of the many trails in Nevada. However, in the context of historical research it is an excellent example of the difficulty in tracing movements and determining geographic locations today. Osmer's report referred to Dunshea Springs. The cadastral survey plat and notes prepared less than two years after Osmer's report spelled the site as 'Dunisher Springs.' Contemporary maps show the name as 'Donna Schee Springs.' The fact that the spelling of a seemingly unique name changed three times emphasizes the difficulty in recreating an accurate historical picture. Of greater difficulty is determining the exact location of sites using more common names. The *Nevada Atlas and Gazetteer,* prepared by DeLorme in 1996, lists thirteen Cottonwood Canyons, thirty-five Cottonwood Creeks, sixteen Rock Creeks, sixteen Table Mountains and forty-nine Willow Creeks, just to name a few. Thus, the locations of some events using these and similar geographic names have been lost.

Donna Schee Springs is approximately nineteen miles north-northeast of the Jungo siding on the occasionally graded back road between Winnemucca and Gerlach.

Dry Creek Station
Lander County

Dry Creek was the site of both a trading post and a Pony Express station. On 21 May 1860, it was the scene of a skirmish typical of many involving such isolated stations. At the time of the fight an Indian woman lived at the station with Silas McCanless. Although the arrangement was by her own choice, this was an extremely tense time in Indian-white relations. Her relatives disapproved of the relationship and sought to bring it to an end. Early in the day fifteen to twenty members of her tribe arrived and demanded that McCanless give the woman to them. Instead he offered them supplies from his trading post and they left. Apparently unsatisfied, they returned to the station and from ambush shot Pony Express man Ralph M. Lozier.[100] Moments later they shot John Applegate, another of the four whites living at the station. Applegate's wound was severe, the ball having entered his thigh, traveling upwards and exiting through his pants pocket. The wounded Applegate, McCanless, and a second Express man, Lafayette 'Bolly' Bolwinkle, retreated into the station house and prepared to defend themselves against the attack.[101] After obtaining a pistol from Bolwinkle, Applegate placed the revolver to his head, bid his comrades goodby and ended the agonizing pain of his wound. Now down to two, Bolwinkle and McCanless realized their chances for survival in the wooden station house were unlikely. Rather than face certain death in the siege they decided to make a run for the Robert's Creek Station thirty miles to the east. Breaking out of the station house they fled on foot. After a short chase the Indians gave up the pursuit of the well-armed pair and returned to loot the station and trading post. The escape was successful, but not without a price. At the beginning of the battle, Bolwinkle had been sleeping inside the station house. In the excitement, he had neglected to put on his boots and made the run barefoot. He suffered cuts, bruises and cactus thorns to his bare feet, but lived to tell the tale.[102] After a week or so the station was reoccupied and the remains of Applegate and Lozier were buried nearby with rocks stacked on the graves to protect them.[103]

The Dry Creek Station is located on private land east of Austin. From Austin take US 50 east to Hickison Petroglyph Recreation Site (a good place to camp overnight). From the turnoff for the campground continue east on US 50 approximately one and one half miles. Turn north on the graded gravel road (Dry Creek Road). Take the left (west) fork at 2.8 miles. you will pass a BLM Pony Express Trail sign. The station is about one mile on up the canyon on private land.

Dry Wells Station
Lander County

This station was used briefly during the early days of the Overland Trail. Touring the west in October 1860, Sir Richard Burton described crossing through the pass as "a long and peculiarly rough divide ... ."[104] Part of the route was particularly rough and the life of the station was short. Services were eventually moved to Mount Airy on a route which could more conveniently accommodate wheel traffic. Being a more direct east-west route, the telegraph line was constructed through this pass and by the Dry Wells site. Nothing remains to indicate the location of the site. In general the station was in the canyon north of Railroad Pass in the Shoshone Mountains.[105]

From Austin go west slightly over one mile on US 50 to State Route 722. Take State Route 722 west eighteen and one half miles through Railroad Pass. At the point where Highway 722 turns toward the south there is a road to the west. Go west on this road less than a mile, watching for an unimproved road to the north. Take the unimproved road one and one half miles north. The Dry Wells Station is in the saddle to your east.

Duck Creek
White Pine County

A series of raids by Goshute Indians along the Overland Trail resulted in an expedition into the heart of their range in the late spring of 1863. Early on the morning of 1 May, Captain Samuel P. Smith, with Company K, 2nd California Cavalry, left Fort Ruby traveling east on the trail. The following morning they arrived at Schell Creek Station some sixty miles away. Hiding there through the day, they moved back into Steptoe Valley that evening and proceeded south along the west slope of the Schell Creek Range. Deliberately using the night to cover their move, they camped the following morning in a canyon about ten miles north of Duck Creek where Shoshone scouts had reported a Goshute Indian camp. Before daylight on the 4th, Smith sent one element of the command across Duck Creek to advance upstream on the south side while the other element advanced on the north side. Dismounted, they positioned themselves on either side of the camp. At dawn the signal was given and the soldiers attacked. With complete surprise on the side of the cavalry the battle was short. Twenty-four Indians were killed and at least two escaped. Private John L. Cree was wounded slightly by an arrow in the back.

Remaining at the battle site, the cavalrymen established pickets and waited in hiding anticipating that other Goshutes might arrive. That afternoon a group of five were observed riding toward the now empty camp. During the mounted attack that followed one soldier was wounded and the five Indians were slain. The next day Company K moved across the Schell Creek Range into Spring Valley to the east.

The battle site is on private land where Duck Creek opens into the Steptoe Valley along Nevada State Route 486 north of Ely, Nevada.[106] Go north from Ely sixteen miles on US 93. Turn right (east) on Route 486 for approximately three miles.

Dun Glen, Camp
Pershing County

The town of Dun Glen was established in 1862 on the east side of the Buena Vista Valley. Initially it was a ranching/farming community pioneered by J. Angus Dunn. In time it served as a focal point for commerce in the area in support of mining at Mill

Rock dugouts at Camp Dun Glen
Courtesy: The Author

City, the Sierra Mining Districts and scattered mines in the nearby mountain ranges. The post office was established 18 July 1865, and remained active until 15 April 1913, when Mill City took over the postal routes. It is shown as 'Chafey' on some maps between 1881 and 1911.[107] The area was first used by a military detachment from Fort Churchill in March 1863. The site did not gain military significance until the spring of 1865, at which time it became vital to operations in the Black Rock Desert and Paradise Valley. Never a built up fort or camp, the military's needs were served by a few rock-lined dugouts, tents, and rented buildings.

From its beginnings, anti-Indian sentiment among settlers in the vicinity ran strong. Indians living in the nearby hills and to the north had an equal dislike for the white settlers and their farming of the natural meadows along the Humboldt River and its tributaries. Through the winter of 1864-65, depredations and confrontations were common. Following a series of Indian raids and thievery in January 1865, twenty-one armed civilians attacked a group of Indians in the vicinity of Cunningham Ranch.[108] Later, in April of the same year, another citizens' group conducted an attack at Cane Springs to the north. The white party boasted of bringing home eighteen Indian scalps.[109] A cycle of attacks and reprisals by each side became the rule.

The killing of several settlers in the Paradise Valley and other depredations in Grass Valley prompted James A. Banks, a prominent Nevada legislator, to seek aid from Major McDermit at Fort Churchill.[110] In response, Captain A.B. Wells was sent with one hundred soldiers from Companies D & E, 1st Nevada Cavalry, to Dun Glen on 4 April 1865.[111] By 7 April, the first military engagement was led by First Lieutenant Joseph Wolverton with troops from Company D, 1st Nevada Cavalry. Five Shoshones were killed in the skirmish.[112]

Fearing reprisal against his own band of Paiutes, Captain Soo met with members of the local militia. According to historian Phillip D. Smith,

> On April 23, 1865 an agreement was drawn up between the Indians and the whites that was completely unprecedented in

Nevada History. Captains John and Soo of the Paiutes, made an agreement with Captains Safford, Usher, Bonnifield and Parkinson to move a portion of the Paiute Nation from the Humboldt to the Carson. This would remove most of the friendly and peaceful Indians who wanted to avoid being caught up in the middle of an all-out Indian War. All Indians found in the Humboldt region one week after the agreement were considered as hostiles and would be killed by the whites.[113]

In reality, there were no funds to facilitate such a move or to feed the Indians if they reached the Carson Sink. Indians already residing in the Carson Sink area resented the impact the agreement would have on their meager existence. A.P.K. Safford and E.F. Dunne moved a few Indians at personal expense. Governor Nye offered to allow Safford and the others to draw on state funds and then later attempt to collect from the U.S. government: however, this did not occur. On 26 April 1865, the *Reese River Reveille* printed the generalities of the agreement. Many Indians either had no knowledge of the agreement or were unable to make the move. In essence this opened the season on all Indians not in the Carson River drainage. (*See* Cottonwood Creek.) What started as a standard military response to the increased Indian depredation evolved into an all-out conflict precipitating the largest campaign of the Indian War in the Great Basin.

By June 1865, the command operating out of Dun Glen was augmented by additional troops from the 2nd California Cavalry under First Lieutenant Henry C. Penwell.[114] By late summer 1865, Dun Glen became the central supply depot for nearly all military activity and expeditions into Paradise Valley, the Black Rock Desert, and the drainages of the Humboldt, Quinn and Owyhee Rivers.[115]

Aided by Soo, Penwell with twenty 2nd California Cavalry soldiers and civilians surprised a group of Indians camped at Table Mountain about thirty five miles southeast of Dun Glen. On 30 August 1865, seven Indian men were killed in the battle. In addition, three Indian women were "accidently" killed. Following the battle Penwell destroyed "large quantities of ammunition and supplies."[116] Showing the media sentiment of the times, the Owyhee, Idaho, *Avalanche* reported of Penwell, "[they] go and hunt them as men would wolves that prey on their stock."[117] On 8 October 1865, Penwell again killed "all of the Indians" in a camp some twenty-five miles south of Dun Glen.[118] The target of these and other expeditions to the north were 'renegade' bands of Indians led by Paiutes known as Buffalo Jim and Black Rock Tom.[119] Their bands were comprised of Paiute, Shoshones and Bannocks that were either unwilling or unwelcome to live in the established Indian settlements. As such they were labeled renegades by both the whites and the peaceful. Through the remainder of 1865 and into the winter of 1866, soldiers from Dun Glen were organized into expeditions that eventually led to the defeat of these so called renegade bands.[120] (*See* Paiute Creek, Leonard Creek, *and* Battle Creek.) Dun Glen was officially used as a military post for the last time in April 1866, by Company L, 1st U.S. Cavalry.[121] The camp was abandoned in August 1866, based on General Order 21, Military Department of the Pacific. Civilian occupation of the area continued for many years.[122]

Nothing remains of this site but the remnants of dugout structures and a few scattered foundations.[123] Take exit 151 from I-80. Go south of the Interstate one half mile to a turnoff on the left (east) side of the road. Take the dirt road to the northeast toward a clearly visible canyon in the mountain range. In about two miles you will pass a windmill on your left (north). This is just a check point to let you know you are on the correct road. Six miles from where you turned off of the paved road you should be in a canyon and see some mounds and a few foundations. You will also see some poplar trees. This is the Dun Glen site. The land status is a mixture of private and public land.[124]

Eden Valley
Humboldt County

On 18 January 1867, Lieutenant John Lafferty with fourteen troops from Company A, 8th U.S. Cavalry, fought a small group of Indians in Eden Valley eighteen miles southeast of Camp Scott.

Two Indians were killed and Sergeant John Kelley was wounded by an arrow in the palm of his right hand.[125]   Eden Valley is southeast of Paradise Valley.

Edwards Creek
Churchill County

Between the Reese River and Cold Springs the Overland Trail has three branches to traverse the Desatoya Range. One skirts the northern edge of the mountains, while the other two use passes within the range. The northern branch runs through the valley of Edwards Creek. Edwards Creek was named by Captain J.H. Simpson, U.S. Topographical Engineers, in 1859, after one of his assistants, Edward Jagiello. In his report Simpson states, "his surname being difficult of pronunciation, I have preferred his Christian name as the appellation."[126] The Pony Express and Overland Stage Station were approximately ten miles north of Cold Springs Station.

Egan Station/Egan Canyon
White Pine County

This Pony Express station was built in the spring of 1860 by Mormon Major Howard Egan. It is also known as Gold Canyon and is on the generalized boundary between Shoshone and Goshute Indian territory. On 16 July 1860, the station was the scene of a major battle with members of the Goshute tribe. Early in the day some eighty Indians had confronted station keeper Mike Holten and rider Henry Woodville 'Slim' Wilson.[127] Demanding food, the Indians consumed everything that was on hand. They then forced the two whites to bake bread with all of the available flour. This done, they tied the two to an upright wagon tongue and prepared to burn them alive. (An alternate account indicates the two barricaded themselves in the station house.) Upon coming in sight of the station, rider William 'Billy' Dennis quickly realized the situation. He wheeled about, and rode back to the west for help. Within minutes he overtook soldiers he had encountered earlier on the trail. Called to the rescue, First Lieutenant Stephen

Cemetery near Egan Canyon Station
Courtesy: Shirley Rathbun

H. Weed, Company B, 4th U.S. Artillery, quickly formed a plan for the rescue. Nearing the station he sent Corporal Mitchell with twenty men to block the Indians' avenue of retreat through the canyon. Concurrently, he prepared to charge the Indians at the station from the west. In the confusion Mitchell rode into the Indian war party, prematurely initiating an intense battle. With no other choice, Weed initiated his charge, but at a greater distance than planned. Many of the Indians escaped to the east through Egan Canyon, but not before leaving eighteen of their group dead on the battle field and abandoning sixty of their horses.

Holten and Wilson survived the battle, but three soldiers were killed and several others were wounded. Mitchell was shot three times, (once in the back) but recovered only to die some six months later.[128] Continuing the epilogue, Weed served the Union forces during the Civil War, rose to the brevet rank of Brigadier General and was killed in action at Gettysburg, Pennsylvania on 3 July 1863.[129]

In a report submitted on 11 August 1860, Company B indicated involvement in several additional battles along the Overland Trail between the Egan Canyon Station and the Deep Creek Station in Utah.[130] In October 1860 after the soldiers returned to Camp Floyd in Utah, surviving Indians returned to Egan Canyon Station. They killed the occupants and burned the station house to ground. On 5 October 1860, Sir Richard Burton made the following entry in his journal,

> Under the circumstances, it was cold comfort to find when we had cleared the canyon that Egan's Station at the mouth had been reduced to a chimney stack and a few charred posts. The Gosh-Yutas had set fire to it two or three days before our arrival in revenge for the death of seventeen of their men by Lt. Weed's party. We could distinguish in the pits from which wolves had torn up the corpses, and one fellow's arm projected from the snow.[131]

Egan Canyon was the site of both white and Indian ambushes throughout its use by Chorpenning's mail, the Pony Express, and the Overland Stage. A contingent of soldiers was frequently assigned to stations on both ends of Egan Canyon for several years.[132] It is located thirteen miles northwest of Schellbourne, Nevada. Turn west on the improved gravel road at Schellbourne. After crossing the Steptoe Valley (eleven miles) the road forks. The right (north) fork goes to Cherry Creek. Take the left (west) fork two miles through Egan Canyon. The station was on the south side of the creek after leaving the canyon. Local tradition holds that the cemetery contains the remains of three soldiers killed in the fight.

Eight Mile Station
White Pine County

On 22 March 1863, the eastbound stage was ambushed by Indians on the Overland Trail a few miles west of Eight Mile Station. The driver was Henry 'Happy Harry' Harper and his passengers included an old man, his two sons, and Judge J.N. Mott from California. As they approached the station the driver was wounded. Mott took control of the horses pulling the coach and was able to outrun the pursuers. Sounding more like a dime novel or the theme from a black and white western movie than a serious text, an early history of Nevada colorfully describes the incident as follows:

> As the stage arrived at the scene of the tragedy it was received by a volley from the savages, who were concealed in and about the house, followed by a war-whoop that once heard is never forgotten. Away dashed the frightened horses guided by the unerring hand of the driver, whose life blood was flowing from a mortal wound. The old man, struck by an arrow, sank to the bottom of the coach-boot unconscious, and the only chance of escape that remained for any of them rested in the nerve, skill and bravery of the hero outside. Clinging to the lines and fighting against the death that was creeping into his vitals, the driver urged forward those maddened animals in his struggle for safety of those whose lives were intrusted [sic] to his charge, until the film gathering in his eyes he called to the Judge to come out and take his place. While the stage was flying at the top of the horses' speed Judge Mott made his way by clinging to the sides of the coach to the driver's assistance, and as he grasped

the lines Happy Harry sank dying under the seat, whence the dark angel summoned him to a place beside the world's forgotten heros.[133]

Without stopping, Judge Mott drove the stage on to Deep Creek Station in Utah. That same day the Indians burned the Eight Mile Station, killed the station keeper and ran off the stock. Also on the 22nd the Schell Creek Station and stage were ambushed. These incidents marked the beginning of what came to be known as the Goshute War.[134]

Upon receiving the report of the attacks Captain Samuel P. Smith with Company K, 2nd California Cavalry, left Camp Douglas, Utah, to follow the Overland route looking for signs of the Indians that had burned the stations. After several weeks in the field they arrived at Fort Ruby in late April without any engagements. Most of the Goshute hostilities against the whites were focused around Eight Mile Station (also known as Prairie Gate and Fort Trinity), Antelope Station to the west, and Deep Creek Station in Utah to the east. Depredations and threats continued. In May 1863, soldiers from Company E, 3rd California Infantry, were stationed at each of the Overland stations from Salt Lake City, Utah, to Austin, Nevada.[135] After resupply at Fort Ruby, Smith resumed his cavalry campaign in early May with much greater success. (*See* Duck Creek and Spring Valley.) Although hostilities were greatly reduced the threat remained and as late as June 1864, Lieutenant Colonel J.B. Moore, commanding the 3rd California Infantry, routinely provided troops at each station and sent soldiers to ride the stagecoach as guards.[136]

To reach Eight Mile Station, go north from Ely on US 93 thirty-seven miles to Schellbourne. Take State Route 2 east ten and one half miles through the pass to State Route 893. Go south slightly over three miles on State Route 2/State Route 893 to a junction where you should turn east continuing on State Route 2. State Route 2 winds through foothills almost five miles to another junction. Turn toward the northeast and continue approximately eleven and one half miles to the Tippett Ranch. From the Tippett

Ranch continue slightly over three miles in a northeasterly direction to a fork in the road. Take the right fork (east) and continue in an northeasterly (occasionally easterly) direction. In about five and one half miles you will enter the Goshute Indian Reservation. Continue an additional nine and one half miles to the Eight Mile Station. You have been following the general route of the Overland Trail since leaving US 93. Much of this route is also the Lincoln Highway, the first transcontinental road constructed for automobile traffic. The relationship of old structures currently at the site to the actual station is unknown.

Camp Number 82
Humboldt County

A temporary camp north of Summit Lake, it was used briefly in 1864.[137]

El Dorado, Camp
Clark County

Originally a small mining town and hideout for those trying to avoid conscription, El Dorado was first settled in 1861.[138] Captain George Price and First Lieutenant George Conrad, 2nd California Cavalry, visited the area in May and again in July 1864 during a reconnaissance of the route from central Utah to Fort Mojave, Arizona.[139]

Never of any military value, the camp is more an example of political manipulation than strategic wisdom. In 1866, that portion of the Arizona Territory west of the Colorado River was added to the existing State of Nevada. Having lost what little influence they had in Arizona, the few residents in the area began directly lobbying the military command in San Francisco for military support. Troubles with the Hualapai Indians across the Colorado River appeared to offer justification for the camp. The site was first occupied on 1 January 1867 by Second Lieutenant James Richard Hardenbergh with forty-nine men of Company D, 9th U.S. Infantry. Their mission was to protect miners in the vicinity from Indian raids.[140] Upon arriving Hardenbergh found only three miners and few Indians, all of whom were friendly and glad to see new faces.[141]

Two weeks later Captain Edmond John Yard, the company commander, arrived from Camp Cady, California, with the company headquarters section (eleven enlisted soldiers). A site was selected about one-quarter mile from the mouth of El Dorado Canyon on the west bank of the Colorado River. After selecting the site, Yard left for a new assignment. In June 1867, Yard's replacement, First Lieutenant Charles Hamilton Shepard, arrived and within days realized the uselessness of the post. He obtained permission to move the garrison to Fort Mojave under the command of Major William Redwood Price, 8th U.S. Cavalry.[142] On 24 August 1867, the majority of the Company D soldiers made the march to Fort Mojave, Arizona.

Hardenbergh remained at Camp El Dorado with a small detachment to man Camp El Dorado and its outliers at Las Vegas (Camp Baker) and Callville (Camp Call). In November, he moved the remaining troops to Fort Mojave. The political aspects were not completely ignored. Responsibility for at least maintaining the illusion of an outpost at El Dorado canyon fell to Company K, 14th U.S. Infantry, stationed at Camp Cady, California. The order discontinuing the outpost at El Dorado Canyon was issued 9 June 1869. The order was linked to reassigning the troops from Camp Cady, California, to the Presidio at San Francisco.[143]

Go south ten miles on US 95 from its junction with US 93 (west of Boulder City). Turn east on State Route 165 and travel eighteen miles to Nelson's Landing. Nelsons Landing is the site of Camp El Dorado. Nothing remains of the dug outs and crude shelters that made up the camp. The land is administered by the National Park Service as part of Lake Mead National Recreation Area.

Elko, Camp
Elko County
A Camp Elko was authorized, but never built.[144]

Fairbanks Station
Humboldt County
Fairbanks station was the focal point for an expedition by

Lieutenant Richard A. Osmer and Company B, 2nd California Cavalry, in July 1865. One of several expeditions originating from Camp Dun Glen, Osmer's detachment left Dun Glen on 4 July 1865. On the 5th, with Lieutenant W.G. Overend and a Mr. Fairbanks, Osmer reported traveling to a mountain range east of Fairbanks Station known as Second East Range (twenty-five miles east of Fairbanks Station). There he "found Indian sign, Indian fortifications, but no Indians."[145] He reported arriving at the Golconda Mountains on the 8th. From there he conducted a search of the Summit Springs area in the Golconda Mountains through the 14th. On the 15th, he moved from Summit Springs to Evans Canyon to continue his search for hostile Indians. From Evans Canyon he sent a squad to search Clear Creek Canyon while he searched through Sonoma Canyon to Grass Valley. He proceeded back to Dun Glen without observing any congregation of Indians.[146]

The exact location of Fairbanks Station is unknown. Fairbanks Creek, a tributary of the Little Humboldt River, is approximately fifteen miles due east of Paradise Valley. Plotting Osmer's movements from other known locations tends to place the station farther to the south. The mountain range referred to by Osmer as the Golconda Range appears to be what is now known as the Sonoma Range south-southeast of Winnemucca. Sonoma Creek, Clear Creek and Grass Valley are on the west face of the Sonoma Range.

Fish Creek
(*See* Leonard Creek.)

Fish Lake, Camp
Esmeralda County

As early as 1865, miners in Aurora urged the establishment of a military post in the Fish Lake Valley. On 9 January 1865, Aurora community leaders wrote to Major General Irvin McDowell describing Indian depredations and stating,

> Montgomery district, in the White Mountains, partly in California and partly in Nevada, and the Columbus district, about thirty miles from Montgomery come within the range of

these roving tribes, and the white men in the vicinity are in constant danger of losing their lives. The present difficulties and danger which these men have to encounter very much check the occupation of these mines and the investments that would be made. There is a place known as Fish Lake, in the vicinity of Montgomery and Columbus districts, where excellent grass, water, and timber abound and the climate mild. The Indians resort there a great deal and could be easily controlled from that point by a military force.[147]

No immediate action was taken on the request other than increasing patrols in the area. However, by 1866, mining exploration increased and so did the need for troops in the area. Soldiers from Camp Independence, California, frequently visited the Fish Lake Valley. Official records show an engagement on 29 July 1866, involving Detachment D, 1st U.S. Cavalry, "east of Owens Lake."[148] In December 1866, a temporary camp was established near Fish Lake. Its mission was to protect miners and settlers from Indians in the White Mountains.[149] Also referred to as the Fish Lake Valley Military Station, little is know about this isolated post. An untitled 1881 map shows a 'Military Station' a few miles southwest of Fish Lake. Land Office surveys from the approximate time of occupation make no indication of military structures or a camp. The site was occupied on a temporary basis from December 1866 to July 1867, probably by troops from Company D, 1st U.S. Cavalry.

Fish Lake Valley is five miles east of Dyer, Nevada, and west of Silver Peak. The exact location of the military post is not documented in the official records, but local residents believe the rock ruins west of the present-day cemetery are the remnants of the military camp. Additionally, First Lieutenant George Wheeler's 1874 survey shows an 'old Military Post' about two and one half miles west of the California-Nevada boundary at the foot of the White Mountains.

Forty Mile Desert Trail
Churchill County
The Forty Mile Desert was reported in many traveler's

journals as the most treacherous stretch on the California Emigrant Trail. It was usually reached in August by emigrants leaving Saint Louis in the early spring. The combined effects of the distance traveled, the weight in often overloaded wagons, and the dry summer heat took its toll. As a result this segment was prominently marked by the bones of dead oxen and goods discarded from the pioneer's wagons. The Forty Mile Desert segment of the trail runs between the Humboldt Sink and Ragtown on the Carson River. Units moving between Fort Churchill, Dun Glen and other northern settlements were required to take this route. Once the crossing was initiated the common practice was to continue through the night. During the summer months this helped to reduce the ravages of the heat on this barren dusty playa.

In 1864, Captain A.B. Wells, with Company D, 1st Nevada Cavalry, reports, "Camp No.2, June 10, left camp at 5 p.m.; traveled a distance of thirty-five miles in a northeasterly direction; arrived at the sink of the Humboldt River at 4 o'clock next morning. This was a complete desert, the whole distance being destitute of wood, grass, and water. Camp No. 3, June 11, laid over one day to rest men and animals, they being much fatigued, as also animals of supply train."[150]

The Forty Mile Desert is the barren playa within the triangle lying generally between Fernley, Fallon, and Lovelock. It is best observed south of I-80 or along US Highway 95 north of Fallon, Nevada.

Friday's Station
Carson City

During the troubled time immediately following the Indian raid at William's Station, fear ran rampant through western Nevada. This became the setting for one of the most remarkable stories of the Pony Express. Carrying the east bound mail for 10 May, rider Robert 'Pony Bob' Haslam left Friday's Station on his normal ride to Buckland Station some seventy-five miles to the east. Upon reaching Reed's Station he found that all of the horses, including his remount, had been claimed for the planned retaliation assault on the Indians at Pyramid Lake. (*See* Pyramid Lake Battle, First.)

After feeding his horse he proceeded on to Buckland Station. The next stop, Williams Station, had been attacked, burned to the ground, and the occupants killed only a few days before. When Haslam's relief rider, Johnny Richardson, refused to take the mail W.C. Marley offered Haslam $50 to continue his ride. Haslam took the offer, changed horses, and proceeded. He switched horses again at Sand Springs and rode thirty-four miles farther to Cold Springs. Finding no relief rider there he mounted yet another horse and raced off to Smith Creek Station. There he met Jay G. Kelly who took the mail and continued toward the east.

Haslam, having just handed off the east bound mail, was now in possession of the west bound mail. There being no relief rider he rested briefly, then remounted, and galloped back toward the west. Upon arriving back at Cold Springs Station he found the Indians had attacked the station during the few hours separating his earlier visit. The station keeper had been killed and there were no livestock to exchange for his weary mount. Knowing the Indians might be laying in wait along the trail he disregarded the danger and raced on to Sand Springs. Luck was his and the ride was uninterrupted. Upon arrival at the station he reported the status and persuaded the station keeper to accompany him on to the Carson Sinks Station. Stopping only long enough to pass news of the trail behind him he continued his ride. Upon reaching Buckland Station there was still no relief. Marley now upped his earlier offer to $100. Haslam accepted and after only a brief rest he was soon in the saddle headed west. His ride did not end until he reached Friday's Station.

In all, Pony Bob Haslam had ridden three hundred and eighty miles. He did so with minimal rest, riding trail-weary horses, and in the face of perilous conditions that frightened away all of his peers. His ride carried him through a barren region nearly devoid of vegetation; down the steep slopes of the Sierra Nevada Range and back up again. Along the route he witnessed citizens arming themselves both for attack and defense. He ignored the warning words of others who were too terror stricken to leave well-fortified stations. He passed through two stations that had been destroyed by determined Indian warriors within hours of his presence; all to carry out his assigned task of delivering the mail. His deeds have no match and he is a hero by any standard.[151]

Friday's Station was named for 'Friday' Burke who held the franchise to operate a station at the top of Kingsbury Grade.[152] The station is located one mile east of the Nevada-California state line near Lake Tahoe.

Genoa Fort (Mormon Station)
Douglas County

Originally established as a Mormon Fort-Trading Post in 1849 by Hampden S. Beatie and Abner Blackburn, a more permanent settlement was established by Colonel John Reese in 1851 about a mile south of the Blackburn site. Named 'Genoa' by Mormon Elder Orson Hyde reportedly because it reminded him of the birthplace of Christopher Columbus. Hyde arrived at the Mormon Fort on 19 June 1855. In 1857 he left Genoa when Brigham Young summoned the faithful back to Salt Lake City to defend against the 'invading' U.S. Army. As he departed, and finding no takers for his $20,000 asking price, he placed a curse on those that would take over his holding, "The [people] will be visited with thunder and earthquake, and with floods, with pestilence and with famine until your names are not known by men." During his visit on 12 June 1859, Captain J.H. Simpson found "28 dwellings, 2 stores, 2 hotels, a telegraph office, and a printing establishment." From 03 April 1860 to 28 October 1861, the Pony Express delivered the mail with a change of horses in Genoa. Apparently Hyde's curse has yet to take affect as Genoa is considered by many contemporary accounts to be the oldest settlement in Nevada.[153]

The original Pony Express station has long since been lost (the curse?), but it was located on the vacant lot near the courthouse across the street from the present-day museum. The site continued to serve the Overland Stage for many years.[154]

Genoa is eleven miles south of Carson City and three and one half miles west of US 395.

Godfrey Mountains
(*See* Tuscarora Range.)

Gold Canyon Station
(*See* Egan Station.)

Granite Creek Station
Washoe County

Granite Creek is the first cool, fresh water available to west bound travelers after crossing the Black Rock Desert playa on the Humboldt-Honey Lake trail. This site was commonly used by the Indians, early explorers, and later by pioneers, freight haulers, and military personnel. The waters from Granite Creek naturally sub-irrigate the meadow to provide forage for livestock. The station originally consisted of a store house, a stone corral, and a sod residence/office. It was established as a stage and freight station ringed by Honey Lake and Truckee Meadows to the west, settlements along the Humboldt River and Paradise Valley to the east, and Boise to the north.

In March 1865, the station keeper and two other employees (A.J. Curry, Cyrus Creel, and Al Simmons) were killed and the station burned by renegade Indians. The attack was driven by the murder of a Paiute a few weeks before by 'Puck' Walden. Walden had simply murdered the Indian without provocation, seemingly as a joke. The attack started with an exchange of gunfire from Indians in the stone corral and the defenders firing through slits in the sod walls of the station house. Bullet holes in the face of the corral as well as the sod house indicate that many shots were fired. The Indians were able to get close to the sod house using the store house as cover. From there they set fire to the roof of the house. Curry died inside the house, either from wounds or from the flames. Creel and Simmons attempted to escape on foot. Running in opposite directions, Creel ran to the south across the playa toward Trego Hot Springs. Simmons ran to the west toward the Deep Hole Station. Tracks on the playa showed that Creel was chased down by three mounted Indians. He was brought back to

Granite Creek Station - Camp McKee, looking across
the Black Rock Desert toward Trego Hot Springs.
Courtesy: The Author

the house, secured to the ground, and burned alive. Simmons did not get far before he was shot. His body was dragged about and then severely hacked.[155] In an obvious display of rage the furniture was shattered; household pots and pans were broken and smashed; and other equipment at the site was shattered, hacked, broken into pieces or burned. Even the dog at the station was killed, skinned and staked out.[156] Whether the raid was a reprisal for the specific murder or a manifestation of the animosity between renegade Indians and portions of the local white population is not known. The incident directly resulted in establishing several temporary military camps at this, and other stations, along the commerce routes in the area. The camp is named for the station and the local geographic features.[157] (*See also* Camp McKee.)

Granite Creek Station is on private land 5.1 miles northeast of Gerlach on Nevada State Route 34. The actual camp site was located near where Granite Creek empties onto the Black Rock Desert Playa.

Gravelly Ford
Eureka County

One of the better crossings on the Humboldt River, Gravelly Ford was widely used by travelers and Indians in the area. It was at this site that James A. Reed of the Donnor party stabbed John Snyder to death during an argument. The quarrel began while the party was 'doubling up' their teams to pull the wagons up a steep incline at the site. After the stabbing, Reed was banished from the party. He made his way separately to California and later organized the rescue for the Donnor party during their winter ordeal in the Sierras.[158]

In August 1861, Shoshone Indians attached an emigrant party of thirteen at Yago Canyon, which connects the Pine Valley with the Humboldt River southeast of Gravelly Ford. In the attack, two Indians captured a ten-year-old girl and killed her. An Indian woman (Maggie) witnessed the attack and identified the attackers later at Fort Ruby. In an early effort at criminal justice they were hanged for their crime.[159] A year later eleven other emigrants (men, women and children) were killed by Indians eight miles east of Gravelly Ford. This led the commander of the 3rd California Infantry, Colonel Patrick Edward Connor, to issue his widely reported order, in August 1862, to "shoot all male Indians found in the vicinity and to take no prisoners."[160]

By mid-September 1862, Major Charles McDermit reported that twenty-three emigrants had been killed at Gravelly Ford. At the time, Connor was at Fort Ruby and a decision was made that he (Connor's troops) "will attend to it."[161] Also, in the fall of 1862,

> ... a party of secessionists of fifteen persons going east were attacked by Indians on the Humboldt, and all but one were killed. I do not think from the information I could gain from the emigrants who came that secessionists have anything to do with the Indian difficulties there. There are Mormons keeping ferries in the neighborhood of the Indian troubles who sell ammunition and arms to them, and if there are any trains worth robbing the Indians are sure to be informed by these scoundrels, and probably a few white men who are rebels to all governments. - A. Brown.[162]

From 29 September to 29 October 1862 Companies H and K, 2nd California Cavalry, undertook a major campaign in the area. Led by Major Edward McGarry the activities are reported merely as "Affairs on Humboldt River."[163] The events constituted one of the worst atrocities committed by the military in Nevada. Given the times and Connor's order to take no male prisoners, little imagination is needed to visualize what actually happened in contrast to the words of McGarry's report.

> This evening (the ninth) some of the command enticed into camp three Indians; two of them were armed with rifles, and the other with bow and arrows. I immediately ordered their arms taken from them, and placed them under guard, intending to retain them until the arrival of my interpreter ... . A short time after their arrest the Indians made an attempt to obtain their arms, and, having succeeded, they resisted the guard and broke and ran a short distance; they were fired upon by the guard and crippled. Fearing that they would escape, and not wishing to hazard the lives of my men in recapturing them alive, I ordered

the guard to fire, and they were killed on the spot ... he [Captain S.P. Smith] came upon a party of about fourteen or fifteen Indians who were armed with rifles, bows and arrows. He surrounded them and took from them their arms. Immediately after, the Indians attempted to escape by jumping in the river. They were fired upon and nine of them were killed. On the same day Lieutenant [George D.] Conrad and party brought in three Indians and an Indian child. Captain Smith returned in the evening with two squaws. Next day Captain [Daniel] McLean returned bringing in one Indian and a squaw. Same day Lieutenant [Cyrus D.]Clark returned with one Indian; another was captured during the evening. The next day, the thirteenth, I told two of the Indians, through the interpreter, that if they would go and bring in Indians who were engaged in the massacre of emigrants I would release them, but if they did not return that night I would kill all of the Indians I held as prisoners in the camp. The next morning, the fourteenth, hearing nothing from the Indians I had sent out the day previous, I put to death four of those remaining, and released the squaws and the child ... . On the next day, the thirteenth [sic], I sent Lieutenants [Darwin] Chase and Conrad with a detachment on the south side of the Humboldt, with instructions as before. They came upon a party of Indians encamped in the mountains, armed with rifles, bows and arrows. They were surrounded and their arms taken from them. The Indians attempted to escape, were fired upon, when eight of their number were killed.[164]

True to Connor's order, all male Indians were shot and no prisoners were brought with McGarry when his command marched to their next assignment. McGarry continued a military career, was promoted twice, and breveted to Brigadier General in 1865. He was eventually removed from command in Arizona, allegedly for drinking on duty. (*See* Camp McGarry.) On 31 December 1867, he committed suicide in his San Francisco hotel room by stabbing himself in the throat with his pocket knife.[165]

Occasional visits by the military maintained order in the immediate area around Gravelly Ford for the next two years. When hostilities flared in 1865, Gravelly Ford became an area of military activity again. In August 1865, Company B, 2nd California Cavalry, camped at the ford.

The company left Gravelly Ford, Humboldt County, Nev., on the second day of August, 1865, on a scout for Indians. Trailed across the mountains 25 miles; came to the river and found a camp the Indians had just left. Followed their trail, killed one, and captured a number of squaws. Returned to camp, scouting down river; found a camp of hostile Indians. Killed two and wounded several more; and in compliance with instructions from Headquarters District of Nevada, left Gravelly Ford on the twelfth [sic] day of August, 1865, for Dun Glen, and arrived there August 21, 1865."[166]

The area served as a rally point for several years until the coming of the railroad and rerouting of commerce routes near the end of the decade.

From exit 261 on I-80 take State Highway 306, go five miles to the railroad crossing at Beowawe. Follow the railroad maintenance road east five and one half miles to Gravelly Ford. There is an Emigrant Trail marker at the site.

Grubbs Well (Camp Station)
Eureka County

An Overland Mail station, used beginning sometime in July 1861, it was also used by the Pony Express in its last few months of operation. In the mid-1860s, while in use by the Overland Stage, soldiers were periodically stationed here to protect the station. The detachment never numbered more than four or five soldiers.

Nothing remains of the site. It is on privately owned land and is located approximately ten miles north of US 50.[167] The turnoff to the north is twenty and one half miles east of Hickison Petroglyph Recreation Site on US 50, or twenty-four and one half miles west of Eureka on US 50. Go nine and one half miles north on 3 Bars Road. Then drive west two miles on an unimproved dirt road to the site. This is a fair weather only road and not suitable for automobile travel. A monument marks the location of the station. The log structure at the site is typical of the architecture of the time but is reported to have been built more recently.

Guano Valley - Rock Canyon
Washoe County

This remote area was the scene of two significant battles near the close of hostilities in Nevada. The isolation of the area made it a natural sanctuary for Indians raiding settlements in north-eastern California, northern Nevada and south-central Oregon. As part of an organized effort against Bannocks, Snakes, and Paiutes, several expeditions were launched from Fort Bidwell and the camp at Summit Lake. (*See* Camp McGarry.) In February 1866, Major Samuel P. Smith, 2nd California Cavalry, commanding thirty-two soldiers from Company D, nineteen from Company F, and some thirty armed citizens moved to the area.

The attack on the Indian camp was made at 9:30 o'clock a.m. of the morning of the fifteenth, the fight continuing till 3:30 o'clock p.m. As the troops charged the camp the Indians retreated into Rock Canon and Bluff. The chief, Smoke Creek Jim, was killed at the commencement of the fight. Found on the field, at the close of the fight, eighty-one warriors. Killed fifteen squaws and papooses in the rocks, it being impossible to distinguish one sex from the other. Fifteen Indians, supposed to be badly wounded, hid in caves and escaped the following night. During the action, nineteen squaws and papooses were taken prisoners, and placed under guard. On breaking camp on the morning of the twentieth, they were set at liberty and supplied with thirty days' rations of dried beef. Captured seventy-five horses, belonging to citizens of Suprise Valley, Cal. The whole Indian camp and equipage, and about three tons of dried beef, were committed to flames. The camp was composed of thirty-five wickiups. The band of Indians was composed of Paiutes, Bannocks, and Snakes, who had been committing depredations in this section of the country for the past four years.[168]

In the battle Smith was wounded. Also, Private Charles Austin of Company D was killed. Corporal George Grimshaw and Privates Edward Resler, Henrich Ruhmann and Frank Belto (of Company D), and Privates Alexander Mills and Charles H. Smith (of Company F) were wounded. All recovered and returned to duty except Belto, who was discharged at Smoke Creek on 8 May as disabled.[169]

above: Camp Halleck. *Courtesy: Nevada Historical Society*
below: Camp Halleck, looking across the parade grounds
toward the Ruby Mountains.
Courtesy: The Author

Lieutenant George H. Robinson, with thirty-three soldiers of Company D, 2nd California Calvary, was left to scout the area and returned on 4 March 1866, without further engagement. This significant battle greatly reduced conflict in the area.

Major Smith recovered from his wounds, mustered out of the California Cavalry in June 1866, and accepted a commission as a captain in the 8th U.S. Cavalry. He was eventually discharged at his own request in October 1870, having served with distinction in California, Oregon, Utah and Nevada.[170] (*See also* Duck Creek, Eight Mile Station, Fort Halleck and Spring Valley.)

Guano Valley, so named for bird deposits, is on public and private land in the northwest corner of the Sheldon National Wildlife Refuge on the Nevada-Oregon border.

Halleck, Camp
Elko County

Camp Halleck's primary mission was to protect workers on the Central Pacific Railroad and travelers on the Hastings cutoff. Captain Samuel P. Smith, Commanding Company H, 8th U.S. Cavalry, established the post 26 July 1867. Named in honor of Major General Henry Wagner Halleck (1815-1872), it was designed and built for one company of infantry and one company of cavalry. Company I, 12th U.S. Infantry, joined the cavalry troops in 1868.[171]

The central parade ground was approximately 200 feet on its north-south axis and 320 feet on its east-west axis. An excellent hospital was constructed 250 feet north of the line of the officer's quarters. Adobe and stockade buildings replaced tents and eventually frame buildings replaced these.

Action around the post was almost non-existent. In the nineteen years of the post's life there were no major engagements and only four minor ones. Most assignments took the soldiers on campaigns many miles away and often in adjacent states. Civilian merchants—quick to take the soldier's merger pay—as well as the cold, boredom, and gambling were the main enemies. Various company-sized units of the 1st, 3rd, and 8th U.S. Cavalry Regiments, as well as the 9th, and 12th U.S. Infantry, regiments were rotated through assignments to the post with apparent regularity.[172]

By 1872, only Fort Halleck and Fort McDermit were garrisoned; Halleck with one company of the 1st U.S. Cavalry and one company of the 12th U.S. Infantry.[173] On 5 April 1879, the camp was redesignated a fort as were many other posts in the west. More as a result of political influence than military need, the post continued its existence until 11 October 1886, when it was closed and transferred to the Department of the Interior.

The site is incorporated into a pasture and private ranch. Nothing remains other than a stone monument and brass plate erected in 1939 by the Daughters of Utah Pioneers. It can be reached by taking the Exit 321 (Halleck) on I-80 east of Elko. Travel approximately eleven miles on State Highway 229. Turn west onto the gravel road at the sign marked 'Lamoille.' This road will turn toward the south and at about five and one half miles it turns sharply toward the west. About one mile from this turn (six and one half miles from State 229) you will come to a rock monument on the south side of the road marking the site of Fort Halleck.

Haven, Fort
Washoe County

Fort Haven was a set of temporary earth works established during the second battle of the Pyramid Lake War. The site was selected by Captain Joseph Stewart, 3rd U.S. Artillery, commanding the federal troops in the battle. It is named in honor of Major General J.P. Haven who served as a volunteer to Colonel John C. Hays in the Washoe Regiment of the Nevada Militia. It was used from 6 June to 15 July 1860.[174] Nothing remains at the site which is located approximately one mile south of Pyramid Lake (two miles north of Nixon, Nevada) on the Truckee River.[175]

Hayes, Camp (Miller's Station - Reed's Station)
Lyon County

Also known as Miller's Station and Reed's Station, it is located on private land approximately eight miles east of Dayton. Nothing remains of the old Station established in early April 1860.

It not only served the travelers on the Carson River branch of the Emigrant Trail it also served the Pony Express and the Overland Stage.[176] In May 1860, militia Major William M. Ormsby passed this way, taking the available horses to carry part of his ill-fated force to the defeat at Pyramid Lake .

Later it was an assembly point for volunteers of the Nevada Militia organized to fight in the second battle of the Pyramid Lake War. A temporary camp was established and named for Colonel John 'Jack' C. Hays, Commander of the Washoe Regiment, Nevada Volunteer Militia. The camp was vacated 26 May 1860. The site is located twenty miles east of Carson City. [177]

Homestead, 'Fort'
Storey County

A 'fort' on the heights between Gold Hill and Virginia City was built in the 1860s by militia at the height of the Indian scare associated with the Pyramid Lake Indian War. On 19 April 1865, it was the gathering place for local residents assembled to mourn the death of Abraham Lincoln.[178] Nothing remains to indicate the presence of Fort Homestead.

Honey Lake Smith's Station
(*See* Williams Station.)

Hooten Wells
Lyon County

Only crumbled rock ruins mark the remains of this Overland Stage and Pony Express Station. On US 95 go almost ten miles south of Silver Springs; then turn east and travel twelve miles.[179]

Humboldt Wells (Wells)
(*See* Cottonwood Canyon.)

Humboldt Sinks
Pershing County

On 3 February 1866, Captain G.D. Conrad with eight soldiers of Company B, 2nd California Cavalry, went from Dun Glen to

Humboldt Sinks to investigate reports of hostile Indians living among the Paiutes in the vicinity. Fearing that the hostiles would cause problems for them, local Indians identified two individuals to the soldiers. Conrad apprehended the two known as Shoshone John and Sacramento Sam. They were disarmed and started on the road back toward Dun Glen. In a situation seemingly common for the time, the two were "killed attempting to escape."[180]

Humboldt Sinks marks the northeast corner of the Forty Mile Desert. It is the last reliable source of water and forage before reaching Ragtown on the Carson River to the west. It is the marsh to the east of Exit 93 on I-80 and is part of the Humboldt Wildlife Management Area managed by the US Fish and Wildlife Service. (*See also* Battle Lakes and Forty Mile Desert.)

Jackson Ranch
Humboldt County

On 16 November 1865, en route to the battle at Leonard Creek, First Lieutenant R.A. Osmer, Company B, 2nd California Cavalry, rested briefly at Jackson Ranch. His command consisted of sixty soldiers, four civilians, Paiute Indian Captain Soo with fourteen warriors, supply wagons, and a mountain howitzer. During the night they moved to the Quinn River where the wagons and cannon were left with a detachment of fourteen men. From there he attacked Leonard Creek (Fish Creek) and returned, arriving "back at Jackson Ranch at dark, distance marched 30 miles and about 15 marched during the fight."[181] From here he returned to Dun Glen.

Take US 95 north from Winnemucca thirty-one miles to State Route 140. Travel west on State Route 140 (toward DeNio) thirty-six miles to the Leonard Creek Road. Where the Leonard Creek Road turns west you should continue south next to the Jackson Ranch. Jackson Ranch is approximately twenty-five miles south-southwest of State Route 140.

Jacob's Well
White Pine

There are questions about when the original station was

established and how long it was used. It was not mentioned in the detailed journal of Sir Richard Burton in October 1860. Whether this was an oversight or he regarded it as inconsequential is unknown. It could be that the stage took the route through Railroad Pass to the north. Other reports indicate it was in service in the waning days of the Pony Express and appears to have been incorporated into the system in July 1860. No more than a rock building and a hand-dug well, it was mentioned in a military report in 1865. Second Lieutenant John Tolles, with a detachment from Company B, 1st Nevada Infantry, reported, "June 15, resumed the march; traveled five miles and came to the overland Mail Route, five miles east of Jacob's Wells Station; thence ten miles to the post [Camp Ruby]."[182] It is believed the site served both the Pony Express and the travelers on the Overland Express route through 1869.[183] The well remained in use for many years serving miners and others in this remote part of the Great Basin. Nothing remains of the station today.

Jacobsville
(*See* Reese River Station.)

Lander County
Colonel Frederick West Lander, U.S. Topographical Engineers, was the principal engineer during construction of the Federal wagon road that became the Central Overland Route from Fort Kearny, Nebraska, across Wyoming, Utah, and Nevada to Honey Lake, California. Lander negotiated a truce with Chief Winnemucca in 1860 to allow use of the road. During the Civil War he returned to the East and became a Brigadier General of volunteers. He died on 2 March 1862, at the age of forty, at Paw Paw Hill, Virginia, of wounds received in battle.[184]

Las Vegas
Clark County
Although the Old Spanish Trail had been in use for many years,

Lieutenant John Charles Fremont, U.S. Topographical Engineers, was the first regular U.S. soldier to document his visit to the springs at Las Vegas. On 3 May 1844, he described it as a "narrow clear stream 4-5 feet deep. The taste of the water is good, but rather too warm to be agreeable."[185] In 1854 Congress appropriated $25,000 for a road through the area from Salt Lake City to the eastern boundary of California.[186] The area was again visited by the military in 1855 when Lieutenant Sylvester Mowry, with fifty troopers of the 1st U.S. Dragoons camped there. With him was James Bean, a Mormon, who set up a colony and station to assist travelers. Mowry left the Army, moved to Arizona and went into the mining business. During the Civil War there were serious questions about his loyalty during the Union reoccupation of Arizona and much of his property was confiscated.[187]

Leonard Creek
Humboldt County

Following the report of First Lieutenant Henry Penwell's failure to dislodge Black Rock Tom at Paiute Meadows, a second force was organized under First Lieutenant R.A. Osmer. On the morning of 12 November 1865, Osmer departed Dun Glen, with sixty men of Company B, 2nd California Cavalry, complete with a mountain howitzer. In addition, two civilians, Tom Rule and a Mr. Swim accompanied Osmer. Rule had been badly wounded by Indians on his way to Idaho the previous summer. Now, fully recovered and armed with a new Henry rifle, he accompanied the expedition seeking revenge against his attackers.[188]

Osmer crossed the Humboldt River at Saint Mary's and proceeded west to Willow Creek Station. There he was joined by the Paiute Indian Scout Captain Soo and fourteen of his warriors. In addition, seven more soldiers temporarily stationed near Willow Creek joined the expedition.[189] They marched north to Donna Schee Springs and after camping the night they continued north to the Jackson Ranch. About 2:00 a.m. on the 17th, Osmer moved his force west a little over five miles to the Quinn River. He left the cannon and wagons with fourteen of his command at the river crossing.

After crossing the river they continued west where Captain Soo reported seeing "smoke of the enemy camp fires some nine miles away to the northwest."[190] In the morning, guided by the smoke, the soldiers were able to come within two miles of the Indian camp before they were observed. The *Humboldt Register* reported, "The only order given by Osmer was 'Come on, boys!' and then with an energy that seemed irrestible, the boys in blue, the citizens, and the friendly Indians, every one for himself, but with admirable system, entered upon the contest—each striving to surpass the others in deeds of daring."[191] In a two-mile mounted charge, the entire force descended on the camp as the Indians scattered to escape. The battle lasted nearly four hours and covered several miles.

At the conclusion of the battle the bodies of fifty-five Indians were found.[192] Osmer's report put the number at one hundred twenty Indians, of which about eighty were bucks.[193] In the battle, Private David W. O'Connell was killed by a gunshot wound in the breast. Sergeant Alexander Lansdon and a Private Moon were wounded.[194] Black Rock Tom was not among the dead and was thought to have escaped with ten other Indians.[195]

An incident that highlights the difference between the soldiers' treatment of Indians and civilian treatment occurred after the battle. A corporal and another soldier had been trying to assist a wounded Indian woman and her six-month-old child. When called to other duties they turned her care over to the civilians. Moments after the soldiers moved away, the civilians shot both the woman and her child before the corporal could return to stop them.[196] Official records give a slightly different account stating, "the Indian allies could not be restrained from a general slaughter ... ."[197] The report carried in the *Humboldt Register* makes no mention of this and only states,

> Six horses were captured from the savages, besides a large amount of plunder taken by them from Bellew's wagon [*see* Willow Springs]—consisting of blankets, clothing, blasting powder, tobacco, hand saws, etc.; together with a number of guns and other arms, and a large quantity of seeds. The friendly Indians assisting Osmer were rewarded with all the captured

Indian horses and all of the other spoils they could pack off, and the rest were burnt with the huts ...[198]

The command arrived back at Dun Glen on the 20th having covered approximately 250 miles in seven days.[199]

Changing geographic names, vague route descriptions, and questionable estimates of distances give rise to some confusion about the location of Osmer's 17 November 1865, battle and Captain Conrad's 12 January 1866, battle. Careful reconstruction of the routes of each command strongly suggests the following. Consideration of terrain features relative to clearly identified points and camp sites in the records strongly supports Leonard Creek (formerly Fish Creek) as the site of the 17 November battle, and Battle Creek as the site of the 12 January battle. This is further supported by the *Humboldt Register* story following the 12 January battle stating, "The Indian camps all destroyed and the wounded all cared for, the command marched to Fish Creek [Leonard Creek], where water could be obtained and camped." From there, the command moved on to Cane Springs.[200]

Leonard Creek and Battle Creek are located on the east face of the Pine Forest Range and the Black Rock Range respectively. To get there take US 95 north from Winnemucca thirty-one miles to State Route 140. Travel west on State Route 140 (toward DeNio) thirty-six miles to the Leonard Creek Road. Turn west on Leonard Creek Road and follow it around to the west side of the Jackson Range. At approximately eight and one half miles, Leonard Creek Road departs almost due west from the main north-south road running along the foot of the Jackson Range. Make this right (west) turn and you will cross over the Quinn River. In eight and one half miles you come to a 'T.' Turn left (generally south) at the 'T.' The road angles back in a westerly direction. Go nine miles to the Leonard Creek Ranch. Battle Creek is another two and three quarter miles to a fork in the road. Take the left branch eight and one half miles to Battle Creek Ranch. Continue eight more miles to Paiute Creek Ranch.

Long Valley
Humboldt or Washoe County

Regimental returns for Company A, 1st U.S. Cavalry, indicate an engagement in Long Valley on 3 Oct 1866. Lieutenant John F. Small led this cavalry force in which eight Indians were killed. There is insufficient information to determine with certainty which Long Valley this might be. Company A, 1st U.S. Cavalry, operated along the Nevada-Oregon boundary during this time period. On 8 September 1867, less than a month before this engagement, Small was breveted to captain for "gallantry in charging a band of Indians, killing or capturing more of the enemy than he had men at Silver Lake, Oregon."[201] This would tend to indicate that the correct 'Long Valley' is somewhere near the Nevada-Oregon border.

Lyon, Camp
Lander County

Camp Lyon is a temporary fort shown on the 1880 Wheeler Survey Maps Index. Almost nothing is known about this site. At best it may have been a temporary camp. It is located approximately twenty miles northeast of Battle Mountain, Nevada.[202]

One possible source of the designation involved a 'Captain' (probably not military) Robert Lyon guiding a wagon train from Joliet, Illinois, to California. While camped along the Humboldt River in June 1850, Indians attacked his party. One of his men was "shot through the heart with an arrow while on picket duty."[203] The next day the man was buried at Gravelly Ford and the train proceeded on to the west where they encountered a second party of whites. Livestock used to pull their wagons had been driven off during the Indian attack. The earlier group decided to burn their wagons and proceed west with Lyon and his party. This occurred about twenty miles from Gravelly Ford and thus is in the locale of 'Camp Lyon.'

Martin Creek Gap
(*See* Cottonwood Creek.)

Massacre Lake
Washoe County

In 1850 an emigrant wagon train was attacked here by Indians from the High Rock Canyon area. Nearly forty of the settlers were killed. Their remains were buried in a common grave. The site is approximately ten miles east of Vya on State Route 8A.[204]

McDermit, Fort (Camp McDermit &
Quinn River Camp No. 33)
Humboldt County

In the mid-1860s Indian bands in north-central Nevada and southern Oregon were divided in their response to white settlement of the Northern Great Basin. While some were tolerant, others were clearly hostile and confronted the whites with violence. By the spring of 1865 this second group had formed a coalition made up primarily of renegade bands of Paiutes, Shoshones, and Bannocks. In May, the Nevada Governor and leaders of the many bands of peaceful Indians reached an agreement. Following the agreement, Lieutenant Colonel Charles McDermit, commanding elements of the 2nd California Cavalry, 1st Nevada Cavalry and 1st Nevada Infantry, was given the mission to subdue or destroy these renegade bands. Additional troops were brought from California and the largest military campaign in the Nevada Indian War was launched.

On 18 July 1865, McDermit reported having almost no contact with hostile Indians since initiating the campaign. He returned to his camp on the Little Humboldt and resupplied. From there he took one hundred and twenty soldiers from various units of the Nevada Cavalry and Company D, 6th California Volunteer Infantry and moved into the Queens (Quinn) River Valley. The command was divided with zones assigned to subordinate units. In two minor engagements the forces killed seventeen Indians. By 2 August, the various elements had killed a total of forty-nine Indians in various engagements. His report on that date indicates his belief that the main body of Indians had apparently left Nevada and moved toward the Snow Mountains in Oregon.[205] He stated

Fort McDermit Adjutant's Office is now a community center for the
Fort McDermit Indian Reservation.

Courtesy: The Author

his intent to follow them into Oregon and began shifting operations farther north. Under his direction Captain J.C. Doughty, 2nd California Cavalry, established Camp No. 33 on the east fork of the Quinn River in early August 1865. This camp would serve as the new supply point and headquarters for continuation of the campaign to the north. However, on 7 August 1865, McDermit was attacked from ambush receiving a fatal wound to the chest.[206] (*See* Quinn River-East Fork.) The campaign continued under the command of Major Michael O'Brien, 6th California Infantry, the next ranking officer in the field at the time. Within a few days the name of the camp was changed to Camp McDermit to honor the fallen commander.

In time, Camp McDermit evolved from a temporary logistics base and field headquarters into a permanent camp. The post's primary mission was to protect travelers on the commerce route between Virginia City, Nevada, and Boise City, Idaho. In addition, it became a center for distribution of provisions to friendly Indians in the region. In the 1870s Sarah Winnemucca, daughter of the noted Paiute Chief, Poito Winnemucca, served there as a hospital matron. The camp was redesignated as a fort on 5 April 1879. The post became headquarters for the Fort McDermit Indian Reservation on 24 July 1889. Only one of the original buildings remains; the adjutant's office on the northeast edge of the original post. This building is currently in use as a community center for the Fort McDermit Indian Reservation.[207]

Fort McDermit is located near the Nevada-Oregon border in northern Humboldt County on US Highway 95. The land is part of the Fort McDermit Indian Reservation and is administered by the tribe. Permission should be obtained from tribal authorities before visiting the site.

McGarry, Camp (Camp Summit Lake)
Humboldt County

The site of Camp McGarry was first visited by the U.S. military during the winter of 1842-43. Lieutenant John C. Fremont, U.S. Topographical Engineers, camped in the area and documented its resources.

In 1844, Captain Levi Scott and Captain Linsey Applegate were attacked here. Their guide, a Mr. Garrison, was killed and Applegate had his arm pinned to his side by an arrow during the attack.[208]

On 23 November 1865, Captain Albert Haun established 'Camp Summit Lake' with Companies D and I, 6th California Infantry. Their mission was to protect the stage line from Susanville, California, to the Owyhee mining camps in southern Idaho. Never intended to be a permanent facility, the camp consisted of tents, a few improvised building, and stables made of willow branches and a thatched roof.[209] The camp lacked the facilities to care for either the soldiers or the stores to support them. The post was characterized more by 'reports of survey' for lost and spoiled stores than for interaction with Indians. This did not change with the replacement of the volunteer forces by regular Army forces.

In 1866, the California Volunteers were replaced by the 9th U.S. Infantry. Although they gave the post a more permanent appearance with stone buildings, the loss of stores to rats, mice and elements continued to dominate reports from the post (lost or damaged—106 lbs flour, 453 lbs of bread, 175 lbs coffee, 69 lbs candles, 18 pounds of rice and one pair of infantry trousers; later, 1000 lbs barley damage by rats and mice).[210] The primary mission remained the escort of the stage and other commerce between Camp C.F. Smith to the northeast in Oregon and Fort Bidwell to the west in California. The post had the additional mission of developing a shorter route to Fort Bidwell. This was accomplished, but limited commerce and more desirable routes sent traffic elsewhere.[211] Most activity in pursuit of Indians was also for nought. Typical, were accounts of patrols and detachments spending days looking for stolen livestock or following up on incidents, all without tangible results (ten men, six days looking for Indians holed up in some caves; thirty-five men, six days trying to recapture stolen horses; chased Indians through snow drifts and foul weather to no avail).[212] The most successful action was in October 1868, when fifteen soldiers and nine civilians, led by a second lieutenant on patrol, came upon a camp of approximately fifty Indians. The Indians fled into the timber, abandoning their camp.

Camp McGarry guard house with the administrative office to the left.
Courtesy: The Author

After a brief chase the soldiers returned to the abandoned camp and recovered nine horses, seven saddles, a pistol, a rifle and various supplies. They also found a letter signed by the Indian agent stating, "There has not been any body of armed Indians on the river. If the whites would speak the truth as well and act with as much fairness as the Indians there would be no danger of trouble."[213]

On 9 September 1867, elements of the 1st U.S. Cavalry under Major Albert G. Brackett were assigned to the post. The name of the post was changed to Camp McGarry in honor of Colonel (Brevet Brigadier General) Edward McGarry. Hostile Indian activity in the area was light, and troops were eventually shifted to Camp Scott several miles to the east. On 18 December 1868, the last elements of the 1st U.S. Cavalry moved to Camp Scott. On 25 March 1871, Camp McGarry was abandoned by Federal troops and turned over to Department of the Interior to serve as a reservation for Paiutes and Shoshone.[214]

At one point in its history, headquarters for the District of Nevada was shifted from Fort Churchill to Camp McGarry. On the map the post appears to be centrally located and the designation made sense 'on paper.' Rock buildings were constructed around an abbreviated rectangular parade ground. Shortly afterwards the entire area was reorganized again and Camp McGarry was redesignated as the headquarters for the District of Summit Lake. In reality, the post was (and is) isolated from populations of either white settlers or Indians. After an inspection team made the difficult passage from Fort Bidwell, California, through High Rock Canyon to the remote Camp McGarry, the Headquarters for the District was shifted to Fort Bidwell.

McGarry was originally from New York and started his military career as a second lieutenant in the 10th New York Volunteer Infantry during the War with Mexico. At the outbreak of the Civil War he joined the 2nd California Cavalry as a major, traveling to Utah with Colonel Connor in 1862. During his service in Utah he was promoted through the ranks to colonel and in 1865 breveted to Brigadier General. After the Civil War he was accepted in the U.S. Army as a lieutenant colonel in the 32nd U.S.

Volunteer Infantry with assignment in Arizona. Alcohol led to his removal and eventual suicide in California on 31 December 1867.[215]

Camp McGarry is probably the most remote permanent military post in Nevada. Start with a full tank of gas and a vehicle in good condition. From Gerlach go northeast on State Route 34 and at approximately eleven miles take the right, unpaved fork, marked 'Soldier Meadows Ranch.' Continue north approximately fifty-three miles to Soldier Meadows Ranch. Continue further north fourteen miles, staying on the most traveled road to Summit Lake Reservoir. Travel around the west and then north side of the reservoir to the Camp McGarry site. The rock walls of two administrative buildings are still standing. Rock rubble also clearly marks the outline of the two barracks buildings on the western edge of the parade ground and the officer's row on the southern edge. The land is part of the Summit Lake Indian Reservation and permission should be obtained before visiting the site.

McKee, Camp (also Granite Creek Station)
Washoe County

After the March 1865 murder of the two Granite Creek Station workers (see Granite Creek) troops were assigned to all stage and freight stations on the Susanville-Humboldt River portion of the Honey Lake Road. Although used earlier by military troops, the name Camp McKee, first appeared in official correspondence in December 1865. This essentially coincides with troops being stationed at Summit Lake (eventually Camp McGarry) some fifty miles to the north. The source of the camp's name is unknown. Never much of a post, one report states, "The tents the men are quartered in here are no longer fit for use being in a worn out and torn condition and we have no tent to cook in."[216] Troops were furnished on a rotating basis from Camp McGarry. Forage was plentiful throughout the warmer months from a large meadow naturally subirrigated by Granite Creek. In winter months, forage was also available adjacent to the hot springs near present-day Gerlach. Records indicate that in October 1866, the military stores were sent to Camp McGarry and the military detachment was reassigned.[217]

Although official records indicate it was closed in 1866, the site was still in use by the military as late as 24 July 1867 when the following report was sent to Camp McGarry, "Sweeny of the 9th Infantry was killed by Jackson about 10 minutes ago. Bates was with him. Sweeny was in the act of raising his gun at the time Jackson fired. Mr. Elliott was present. I have Jackson and Bates under arrest. What shall I do with the body and the prisoners? The weather is warm." The record of the reply was not found. Camp McKee and Granite Creek Station were abandoned in 1868 as a stage stop when the road was rerouted.[218]

The site is located on private land approximately five miles northeast of Gerlach on Nevada State Route 34. The actual camp site was located near where Granite Creek empties onto the Black Rock Desert Playa.

Miller's Station
(*See* Fort Hayes.)

Mormon Fort
(*See* Fort Baker-Fort Las Vegas.)

Mormon Station
(*See* Genoa, Fort.)

Mount Airy
Lander County
A station on the Overland Trail, Mount Ariy was used occasionally by the Pony Express when inclement weather prevented use of the route through the mountains to the south.[219] The exact site of the station is unknown. The general locale of the station is given as seventeen miles east of Austin on US 50.

Mountain Springs Station
White Pine County
Mountain Springs Station was used jointly by the Pony Express and the Overland Stage. It was most likely built in July

1861. None of the original structures remain. Today a dam contains the waters of the spring for use by livestock, antelope, and deer in the area.[220] After the Overland Stage stopped running in 1869 the site was abandoned as a station.

The site is located on private lands in the Maverick Springs Mountain Range fifty-one miles north of US 50. The site is not accessible from improved roads.

Mud Lake (Winnemucca Lake)
Washoe County

After receiving reports of a band of Smoke Creek Paiutes rustling cattle in the vicinity of Pyramid Lake, Captain Almond Brown Wells, in command of Company D, 1st Nevada Cavalry, moved to the area. Arriving at the Pyramid Lake on the evening of 13 March 1865, Wells learned that the hostile band was operating from a camp about eleven miles to the north on Mud Lake (present-day Winnemucca Lake). At 3:00 a.m. he moved with twenty-nine soldiers and two civilian guides (W.H. Wilson and T.W. Murch) toward the Lake. His intent was to surround the camp and arrest the Indians for trial in a civilian court. Arriving in the vicinity of their camp at about 5:30 a.m. on the morning of the 14th he divided his group into three squads; Sergeant R.D. Wadleigh on one flank and Sergeant H. Besat on the other, with Wells and ten men in the center. When they were within a few hundred yards of the camp the Indians became aware of the soldiers' advance and fired on them. Corporal John Dolan was wounded in the shoulder. Another musket ball ripped through Well's coat. With the Indians having fired the first shot Wells drew his saber and ordered a charge.[221] All three elements converged in a half circle on the camp. A running battle that covered nearly ten miles on horseback followed. Although ridden by excellent horsemen the Indian ponies were no match for the larger mounts used by the cavalry. When the battle was over the only casualty to the soldiers was the wound suffered by Corporal Dolan. The Indians lost twenty-nine. It was reported that one Indian escaped.[222] In his report, Wells concluded by saying, "After the battle, Winnemucca, chief of the

Pi-Utes, called on me and expressed himself as highly pleased with the result. He told me through the interpreter that he had been talking to them all winter, teaching them not to steal the white men's cattle, and he thought that the punishment they had received would teach them a lesson."[223]

The feeling was apparently not universal among Indian leaders. In the aftermath, other Indian leaders demanded an investigation. Regional newspapers took opposite sides regarding Wells conduct. The Virginia City *Daily Union* and *Gold Hill News* took the view that the attack was unprovoked, unjustified and a violation of the policy of peaceful intervention by the military. To the contrary, the *Territorial Enterprise* supported the captain's actions. Major Charles McDermit reviewed the issue and ultimately decided in Wells' favor. The fact that Corporal Dolan had been wounded during the movement toward the Indian camp was the deciding factor. Less than a month later the Unionville *Humboldt Register* reported that Wells and his command passed through the area on their way to Paradise Valley. The paper described him as, "... a modest, civil fellow—and we wouldn't be afraid to go on a fishing excursion in his neighborhood. [The Soldiers] behaved well while here—no complaint whatever could be heard from them. Before cooking their supper, almost every man took a bath in the creek. 'Cleanliness is akin to godliness'—and we don't believe these fellows will disturb any godly sort of Indian."[224]

Today Mud Lake is known as Winnemucca Lake. It is the large playa on the east side of State Route 447 fifteen miles north of Nixon, Nevada.

Noble's Cutoff/Honey Lake Wagon Road
Pershing and Washoe Counties

Noble's Cutoff was a spur from the California Emigrant Trail to settlements in northern California. During the Indian Wars, the trail was referred to as the Honey Lake-Humboldt Road. From east to west it included stations at Saint Mary's, Willow Creek, Rabbit Hole, (Trego) Hot Springs, Granite Station (Camp McKee), Deep Hole, Wall Springs, Buffalo Slough, and Smoke Creek Station.[225]

All of these stations were involved in the violence of the Indian Wars. Using present-day landmarks, the trail crosses the Humboldt River near the upper reaches of Rye Patch Reservoir; runs generally west to Trego Hot Springs; crosses the western end of the Black Rock Desert; crosses State Route 81 north of Gerlach; skirts the northern edge of the Smoke Creek Desert; and proceeds west-northwest up Smoke Creek into California. The trail has been commemorated with a series of 'T'-shaped railroad rail markers placed by the Oregon-California Trail Association.

Nye, Camp
Carson City

There are two locations for Camp Nye. The first was a temporary camp near the south shore of Washoe Lake. On 6 June 1862, Captain George F. Price established the first Camp Nye five miles north of Carson City. It was used by approximately one hundred troopers from Company M, 2nd California Cavalry. Although this camp site was used less than a week, much of the literature continues to carry this location as the only site for Camp Nye. The camp was named for Governor James W. Nye.[226]

The second site is on the west side of Carson City. On 19 October 1864, Major Milo George was ordered to find a suitable location to establish "comfortable hutting" for two companies of cavalry in the vicinity of Carson City. A parcel of land owned by Henry Koehn was agreed upon. The agreement with Mr. Koehn allowed the military to occupy the site in exchange for the manure from the stable and possession of the buildings when the Army pulled out. At its peak, the post was comprised of six log barracks and two hospital tents. On 23 October 1864, Companies D and E, 1st Nevada Cavalry, left Fort Churchill to occupy the site. The site remained in use until it was ordered abandoned on 29 August 1865.[227]

Nothing remains of the post. The site is currently used by the Carson City Water Department for one of their facilities at the mouth of Kings Canyon. The legal description is SW1/4 NW 1/4 Section 13 T15N, R19E.

Old Spanish Trail
Clark County

The trail was first documented in March 1776 as the route of Fray Francisco Garces when he crossed southern Nevada en route from New Mexico to the California missions. In January 1830, Antonio Armijo used this route to establish commercial trade between Santa Fe, New Mexico, and Los Angeles, California. The earliest detailed military report was made by John C. Fremont as he passed along the route from west to east from 30 April (Stump Spring) to 4 May (California Crossing) in 1844. The route was used heavily by emigrants to Southern California. The most difficult stretch in Nevada was from the waters of the Muddy River to the springs at present day Las Vegas, a distance of approximately fifty miles with no reliable water sources.

From east to west the route generally runs parallels to and south of I-25 along the Virgin River (Mesquite, Bunkerville), then cross country to the junction of Meadow Valley Wash and the Muddy River (near Glendale). From there west to the springs at Las Vegas, Cottonwood Springs (Blue Diamond), Mountain and Potosi Springs (near State Route 160) to Stump Spring and then on to Tecopa Springs, California. Other than in urban and culti-vated areas, the majority of the route is on public lands administered by the Bureau of Land Management.

Ormsby, Camp
Washoe County

This temporary camp, used in May and June 1860 during the second Pyramid Lake Indian War, was named for Militia Major William M. Ormsby who was killed in the first battle. Nothing remains to indicate the location of the site on the Truckee River ten miles south of Pyramid Lake and seven miles south of Nixon.[228]

Otter Creek, Camp
Humboldt County

The official returns for 30 June 1865, show the location of Company I, 2nd California Cavalry, as "Camp No.16, Otter

Creek, Nev."[229] Herbert Hart (see bibliography) shows a very generalized location for this site on his 1965 map. No other reference or information was found on this site.

Overend, Camp
Humboldt and Pershing Counties

This temporary camp was named by First Lieutenant R.A. Osmer, Company B, 2nd California Cavalry, while in command of a detachment sent to scout for hostile Indians believed to be in the Sonoma Range. It was named for his subordinate, Second Lieutenant W. Gibson Overend, a member of the detachment. The camp served as a temporary base in 1865 during the pursuit of roving hostile bands. The few structures were constructed of willows and bark, mainly for protection from the elements. The only effect of the expedition was to keep the Indians on the move. The exact location is unknown but is generally southwest of present-day Golconda in the Sonoma Range.[230]

Overland Stage Route/Pony Express Route
White Pine, Eureka, Lander, Churchill, Lyon, Carson City and Douglas Counties

The Overland Trial was used by a variety of enterprises, including such notables as the Overland Stage Line; The Holladay Overland Mail and Express Company; Wells, Fargo and Company's Express and the Pony Express. Thirty-three stations were established in support of the Overland Stage to California. The Post Office Department awarded a four-year contract at $13,500 per year to make monthly deliveries of mail over this route beginning 1 July 1854. Service was generally intermittent and unreliable. For a variety of reasons the contract was canceled in 1857. By then the route was commonly used for commerce and other public needs. The route was mapped in 1859 by Captain J.H. Simpson, U.S. Topographical Engineers. In the 1860s continued use of the route required a military presence. This condition continued until completion of the railroad altered the lines of communication in the late 1860s. Stations were located at intervals between eight to eighteen miles apart. Many, but not all, of the stations were jointly used by the Pony Express.[231] Appendix B shows the stations of the Overland Trail. The military's role was to provide protection of the mail, emigrants, freight and settlers along the route. The route generally runs close to US Highway 50 from Carson City as far as Austin. From Austin the trail generally parallels US 50, but runs several miles to the north. Much of the trail and many of the stations have been marked with signs or monuments.

Pahranagat Valley
Lincoln County

The valley was named for the Southern Paiute band living in the area. In addition to hunting and gathering, this band cultivated the fertile valley soils using several miles of canals and ditches in their farming. They produced a variety of crops including melons and squash as well as some wheat and corn.[232] A few whites passed through the area as early as 1849 including an ill-fated party that struggled across the barren Death Valley farther to the west.[233] Prospectors dotted the adjacent hills, but richer areas to the west were more attractive. In 1865, there were only seven whites living and prospecting in the valley and adjacent hills. With a few minor exceptions Indians and whites co-existed peacefully.

The most serious incident occurred late in the summer of 1865. W.H. Sales, Indian Agent in the area, failed to deliver goods promised as part of an early agreement. The Indians organized a war party to take what they believed to be rightfully theirs. Forewarned, the few whites packed three wagons and began an escape to nearby Mormon settlements. From Logan in the northwest part of the Valley, the white party moved with their wagons to Crystal Springs. The next morning they traveled to a spring in the saddle between the North and South Pahroc Ranges. There the Indian war party overtook them. In a well-organized plan the Indian force divided into three groups; one to take the livestock; one to block the whites from a nearby spring; and one to confront the camp. The encounter turned into a standoff with the whites holding some Indians hostage while the remaining Indians surrounded the

camp. Intervention by Indians friendly to the white party prevented bloodshed and produced a settlement. In exchange for the
Indian hostages and the goods the whites had with them, the
hostile Indians would allow safe passage. Within months order
was restored and the area returned to a peaceful co-existence.[234]
Other than a few isolated incidents randomly initiated by both
sides, there were never any serious hostilities.

The Pahranagat Valley lies generally along US 93 south of
Hiko and Crystal Springs in Lincoln County approximately one
hundred miles north of Las Vegas.

Paiute Meadows/Paiute Creek
Humboldt County

In 1865 the Paiute chief Black Rock Tom had been raiding settlements and travelers in northern Nevada for several months.[235] In
November, reports were received that his camp had been located on
Paiute Creek adjacent to the east arm of the Black Rock Desert.
First Lieutenant Henry C. Penwell went into the field from Dun Glen
with twenty-six troopers of the 2nd California Cavalry to find and
destroy the camp. Concerned that Black Rock Tom's raids on the
whites might lead to reprisals against peaceful Indians, Indian
Captain Soo guided the soldiers to the area of Tom's campsite. On
9 November 1865, as the soldiers moved up Paiute Creek, the Indians
attacked. Where the deep canyon narrows, steep rock walls provide an easily defended position against the soldiers. The heavy fire
from the well-concealed Indians forced Penwell to withdraw. After
repeated attempts to dislodge the Indian force, he moved about
seven miles out into the Valley to regroup and camp for the night.
Aware that they faced a large, well-armed force, the lieutenant
decided to return to Dun Glen to organize a second offensive.
Arriving at Dun Glen on the 13th, Penwell made his report and a
larger force was immediately assembled.[236] (*See* Leonard Creek.)

Paradise Valley
Humboldt County

In the 1860s, the hills and canyons surrounding Paradise Valley provided natural resources in an abundance not common to the rest of Nevada. Wood, pine nuts, native grass seeds, and game birds, as well as deer, and antelope offered many of the components to sustain the Indian life style. The rich soil and numerous streams also made the area suitable for the more intensive cultivation common to the white culture. Competition for these resources in an otherwise bleak landscape led to some of the most brutal and determined fighting in Nevada.

The first occupation by whites was in June 1863, when W.C. Gregg established a cabin and cut roughly 250 tons of wild hay which he then sold in Star City.[237] By the spring of 1864 at least fifteen farms had been established and native meadows gave way to cultivation. Families in sod and willow huts began to appear where Indians had harvested seed from native grasses and hunted game. The farmers' harvest brought high prices in the mine towns and more land was cultivated. A collision of cultures was imminent.[238]

Prior to 1864, conflicts between whites and Indians were uncommon; particularly during the summer and early fall months. The general exception were attacks on prospectors and travelers in the mountains and foothills. They were at risk from attack by either nomadic Indians or white bandits without regard to season. In winter and early spring, when the natural harvest was at its lowest, conflicts were more frequent. As settlement increased in the valley so did attacks on these isolated farms and ranches.[239] On 21 June 1864, Captain A.B. Wells with Company D, 1st Nevada Cavalry, led the first recorded military patrol into Paradise Valley. His mission was to follow up on the massacre of a group of settlers by Paiutes.[240] The expedition was without incident and Wells' presence seemed to ward off other attacks for a while.

In 1865, Paradise Valley became the focal point for the largest military expedition of the Indian War in the Great Basin. On 4 April 1865, friendly Indians warned settler Aaron Denio that in "two sleeps" warriors would kill all Paradise Valley settlers.[241] Thus alerted, many of the settlers gathered for their own safety at Willow Point to the south.[242] The Indian attack took place just as the friendly Indians had warned. For the next few weeks soldiers of Company

D, 1st Nevada Cavalry, were able to defeat or chase away many small Indian groups.[243] However, this was the beginning of a pattern of depredations on isolated white settlements and stations throughout north-central Nevada that would continue for several months.

Indian attacks were followed by cavalry or civilian counterattacks. Often the whites made little distinction between guilty and innocent Indians. Sentiment among the Indians was split, some desiring peace and others determined to defeat the whites or die in the attempt. Intense military activity (provoked or otherwise) along the Overland Trail farther to the south led many Indians to move into the remote hills and mountain ranges around Paradise Valley. A coalition of those desiring war was growing. Unaware of this, Company D, 1st Nevada Cavalry, narrowly escaped two near disasters farther to the east during engagements in May 1865.[244] In the Tuscarora Range, twice they were forced to retreat under overwhelming fire twice by a large, well-armed Indian force. At Fort Churchill and in Carson City a decision was made to obtain additional troops from outside the District of Nevada and wage a major campaign to defeat these Indians.

After reaching an agreement with those Indians desiring peace Lieutenant Colonel Charles McDermit, commanding most of the troops in northern Nevada, established his operational headquarters in Paradise Valley on 10 June. Under his immediate control were 237 soldiers and two howitzers. Wagons, supplies, and lines of communications were positioned to support operations as long as might be necessary.[245] From this valley, McDermit divided his command into four elements. One to patrol the Humboldt and Reese River area to the south; another to cover the Queens (Quinn) River area to the west, and the remaining two to converge from different directions on selected areas to the east. Over the next several months the campaign succeeded in dispersing the Indian coalition. Once the Indians were reduced to smaller isolated bands they were defeated in Nevada in a series of company-sized engagements.[246]

Hostilities continued, but far less often. One of the last engagements for a volunteer unit occurred on 7 March 1866. Sergeant James T. Brown with an eight-man detachment from

Company I, 2nd California Cavalry, killed six Indians with no losses to the soldiers. Many of the remaining Indians were not prone toward war, and on 18 May 1866, the 2nd California Cavalry escorted one hundred twenty Indians to Fort Churchill, then commanded by Major A.G. Brackett, 1st U.S. Cavalry.[247] Having been relieved by regulars, the last of the volunteer units mustered out by the end of the year. Camp Scott was established in December 1866, by regular troops, who then picked up the mission of protecting the area from the few renegades still operating from the hills surrounding the valley.

Paradise Valley is on Nevada State Route 290 approximately thirty-nine miles north of Winnemucca. In the context of early Nevada history Paradise Valley includes the drainage basin of the Little Humboldt River. (*See also* Camp Scott)

Penrod Hotel Fort
(*See* Carson City.)

Pollock, Camp
Washoe County
Varying reports of its location indicate that Camp Pollock was not a fixed camp, but rather the name given to the constantly shifting supply trains (wagons) for the 2nd California Cavalry and the 1st Nevada Cavalry. In most field operations soldiers rarely carried more than one or two days rations. Ammunition was also limited to an amount sufficient for one or two engagements. Additional supplies, tentage, and other equipment were carried on the wagons assigned the company. Each company had two teamsters and a wagoneer as permanent members of the unit.[248] In addition to carrying supplies, at least one wagon on each expedition was often equipped with an odometer. This accounts for the more accurate mileage reports when wagons were part of an expedition. Occasionally, the higher commanded furnished additional wagons for specific missions of longer duration.

The practice of individual soldiers carrying their 'basic load' and obtaining quick resupply from the 'trains' in the vicinity of the operation is still in use today. The trains (*e.g.* Camp Pollock and Camp Black) also served as temporary aid stations for sick or wounded soldiers. The trains were also a place to treat injured horses, repair equipment, and perform administrative tasks. Commonly the surgeon, farrier, saddle maker and other non-combatant soldiers were found with the trains. The services available and amount of supply were normally tailored to the mission. In the report of his summer expedition in 1864, Captain A.B. Wells, commanding Company D, 1st Nevada Cavalry, reported losses at Camp Pollock as one soldier having died of disease and eight others deserted.[249]

Camp Pollock was reported to be on the Nevada-California State line, near Warm Springs; in the western end of the Black Rock Desert; and southwest of the Smoke Creek Station.[250] Never a permanent camp, it was named after Colonel Robert Pollock of the 3rd California Infantry. Camp Pollock was used from 26 June to 19 July 1864.[251]

Pyramid Lake Indian Reservation
Washoe County

In April 1860, chiefs from the several bands of Paiutes held council at Pyramid Lake to discuss courses of action relative to the increasing number of whites settling in their respective areas. The discussions were heated and the Indians were split in their positions. Some favored all-out war while others sought peaceful solutions.

Chief Qu-da-zo-bo-eat, a Shoshone married to a Paiute, was for war. From as far away as Powder River, half-Bannock and half-Paiute Chief Sa-wa-da-be-bo also favored war. We-he (*see* Walker Lake), a brother of Old Winnemucca favored war as did Sa-a-Ba, Smoke Creek Desert chief and brother-in-law to Old Winnemucca. No-Jo-mud, Honey Lake Chief, and his lieutenant, Ho-zi-a, both favored war. Yurdy, from the bend in the Carson River to the south wanted war. Ha-za-bok from Antelope Valley favored war and offered to supply bullets; "by changing their tobacco into lead; to cause the ground to open and swallow the

Young Chief Winnemucca.
Courtesy: University of Nevada-Reno Library

whites; and to kill them with fierce storms of hail."[252] Se-quin-a-ta, an older Black Rock Chief still living from Captain John Fremont's 1844 visit, favored war. Po-I-to, known as Old Winnemucca, was the chief over all and medicine chief of the tribe. Po-I-to, giving the illusion of objectivity, took no position, declaring instead that he was neither for peace nor war.

Most outspoken in favor of war was the chief from Big Meadows (Lovelock vicinity), Mo-guan-no-ga. During the discussion his patience gave way to action. He left the council with several of his warriors and rode to the station on the Carson River owned by James O. Williams. Several young Paiute women were known to be held captive there. Mo-guan-no-ga, later known to the whites as Captain Soo, and his warriors killed the occupants and freed the Paiute women. Concurrently, several miles to the northwest in the vicinity of Honey Lake, John Gibson and seven other settlers were killed and their houses burned. These coordinated attacks were an attempt to show other Indians their power and gain unanimity in favor of a general war against the whites.[253]

Numaga, known to the whites as Young Winnemucca, was adamantly opposed to war. Having lived with the whites and fully aware of their number, their weapons, and their great armies, he had voiced his opposition throughout the council. Although credited as the overall Paiute war chief by the whites, he was only chief for those Indians living on the Pyramid Lake Reservation. His influence came from his intelligence and ability to express his thoughts. Other Indians told him, "Your skin is red, but your heart is white; go away and live with the pale-faces."[254] He is quoted as responding,

> The white men are like the stars over your heads. Your enemies are like the sands in the bed of your rivers; when taken away they only give place for more to come and settle there. They will come like the sand in a whirlwind and drive you from your homes. You will be forced among the barren rocks of the north, where your ponies will die; where you will see the women and old men starve; and listen to the cries of your children for food.

The story goes that even as Numaga gave his warning and foretold the future, an Indian rider came in and told of the raid by Mo-guan-no-ga on Williams Station. Numaga is said to have responded, "There is no longer any use for counsel; we must prepare for war, for the soldiers will now come here to fight us."[255]

The epilogue for the chiefs is sad tale. Most were to die, not at the hands of the soldiers, but rather would be killed by their own people. Sa-Wa-da-be-bo was the only chief at the counsel killed by the whites. Qu-da-zo-bo-eat was killed by his own people near Battle Mountain. He had been stealing livestock from the whites in Paradise Valley. Members of his band were afraid that he would eventually lead the white soldiers to their camp.[256]

In the spring of 1861, We-he joined a large gathering of Paiutes on Walker River. He gained power by claiming to be a 'spirit chief' and as such was mystically protected from the weapons of his enemies. We-he was attempting to rally support for an attack on Fort Churchill. With help from Indian allies, Indian Agent Warren Wasson was able to defuse the plans and We-he went to Oregon to live among the Bannocks. In May 1862, he returned and again tried to stir up trouble. He was killed by two Paiute chiefs who did not believe his 'spirit chief' claim. To guarantee that he would not rise up from the dead, We-he's body was cut into small pieces and scattered to several distant places.[257]

Chief Sa-a-Ba. was killed by one of his tribe when the chief tried to bewitch him. No-Jo-mud was also killed by his followers for his active hostility toward the whites. Like Qu-da-zo-bo-eat's people, they were convinced that Sa-a-Ba's ways would bring the wrath of the white soldiers to their camp. Ho-zi-a was killed in a take-over of the band by Indian Captain Dick who became the new chief.[258]

Mo-guan-no-ga, later known as Captain Soo, was killed by his own brother. Soo and his cousin, Captain John were arguing about Soo having helped the white soldiers. Soo's brother, Bob, proposed to settle the argument by shooting them both and whichever survived had stronger medicine and would be the chief. He promptly shot his brother, Soo, who then died. John, with medicine at least 'stronger' than Bob's, shot Bob before the thinly veiled coup was completed.[259]

Many Indian names were difficult for whites to pronounce. As a result, contemporary newspapers and historians gave them white names. Short Christian names (*e.g.* George, Tom, Sam, John) were common. These names were not always known to the bearer and the correlation between the name and the deed was not always made. As a result, the deeds of one are sometimes confused with those of another, thus confusing the record and denying the individual their rightful place in written history. The Pyramid Indian Reservation is east of Reno at Nixon.

Pyramid Lake Battle, First - May 1860
Washoe County

Following the attack on Williams Station there was an outcry for reprisal. An earlier request for federal troops had been turned down. There being no regular military in Nevada, civilians in Carson City and surrounding towns armed themselves and set out to defeat the Indians. Their plan was to strike terror in those Indians that would contemplate war with the whites. "An Indian for breakfast and a pony ride" was the slogan for the confident force. Loosely, under the leadership of militia Major William M. Ormsby of Carson City, Thomas Condon, Jr. of Genoa, Richard Watkins of Silver City and Archie McDonald and F. Johnson of Virginia City, a force of one hundred and five men was organized. They assembled at the Delta Saloon in Virginia City. From there they marched to a campsite on the Carson River near present-day Fort Churchill. The following day, carrying nearly as much whiskey as gun powder, and confident that the Indians would not fight such a force, they moved overland to a campsite on the Truckee River near present-day Wadsworth. On the morning of 12 May 1860, they advanced north down the Truckee River to attack the Paiute village. Unknown to the white force, the Paiutes were ready. To the complete surprise of the militia, the Indians flawlessly executed a well-planned defense and counter attack. Using decoys, deception, and maneuver, the Paiutes lured the mounted troops at the head of the column into an ambush away from the river. At the same time the foot troops were drawn into an extended column.

Once dispersed they were easy targets for the numerous Indians who attacked along the flanks. The militia force never regained control or formed an organized defense. Using a few rifles, but mainly bows and arrows the Indians drove their white attackers into a chaotic retreat. Ormsby was with the group of mounted militiamen. In the first few minutes of combat he was shot in both arms and the mouth. Still mounted, he retreated with the few others that managed to escape the initial attack. Richard Watkins rode beside him helping him remain in the saddle. At Ormsby's urging Watkins left him to ride ahead in a vain attempt to rally others into a defense. Ormsby was thrown from his horse and, turning to his pursuers, one of whom he recognized by name, he pleaded to be given a chance to make peace. As he stood in the trail he was shot with two more arrows; first in the stomach and then in the face. There he died from his wounds.

Of the one hundred and five men in the white force, seventy-six were killed. Most of them fell within the first half hour of the battle. Others were killed as they fled back upstream in complete panic. A few of those that survived did so by hiding until darkness covered their escape. Had the battle begun earlier in the day it is likely that there would have been no white survivors. Months after the battle the Indians put their losses at three warriors wounded and two horses killed.[260]

The battle was fought along the east side of the Truckee River in the vicinity of Nixon on the Pyramid Lake Indian Reservation. A highway marker on State Route 447 approximately seven miles south of Nixon commemorates both battles.

Pyramid Lake Battle, Second - June 1860
Washoe County

Ormsby's defeat in mid-May 1860 mobilized citizens not only in Nevada, but in neighboring communities in California as well. By the end of May, 544 volunteers had answered the call and were organized into seven cavalry and nine infantry companies. On 31 May 1860, Colonel John C. Hayes assembled his force on the Truckee River near present-day Wadsworth. There they were joined by two hundred and eleven soldiers of the U.S. Army under Captain Joseph M. Stewart. The regular Army contingent was made up of Stewart (commanding) with eighty-two men of the 3rd U.S. Artillery, Second Lieutenant Horatio Gibson, 3rd U.S. Artillery with howitzers and ten men; Captain Franklin F. Flint with sixty two men from Company A, 6th U.S. Infantry, and Lieutenant J. McCreary with fifty-three men from Company H, also of the 6th U.S. Infantry. Captains Tredwell Moore and Ed Byrne served as Quartermaster and Assistant Quartermaster respectively and Charles C. Keany served as Surgeon.[261]

On the morning of 2 June, two groups of forty mounted militia, each under militia Captains J.B. Van Hagan and E.F. Storey scouted north on the Truckee River toward Pyramid Lake. They soon encountered about three hundred mounted Paiutes riding toward them from the direction of Pyramid Lake. An equal number was advancing on foot. True to their orders to avoid an engagement, they conducted an orderly withdrawal down the west side of the Truckee. Upon seeing Hayes' force, the militia cavalry turned about and began to engage the oncoming Indians. Hayes' men formed an east-west line, as did the Indians, with both forces extending about a mile from the river. The battle lasted nearly five hours with the militia and regulars moving forward inch by inch as the Indians slowly gave ground. In time, the Indians withdrew back to the north. The number of white casualties is unclear, but appear to be four militia killed, a like number wounded, and four regulars wounded with none killed. Militia cavalry Captain Storey was among the whites killed. Reports of Indian casualties vary from a high of one hundred and sixty killed and many more wounded to the low of four killed and seven wounded. With the Indians having been dispersed, the volunteers were released on 7 June.[262] The U.S. Army soldiers remained in the area to provide general security.

The battle was fought along the west side of the Truckee River south of Nixon on the Pyramid Lake Indian Reservation. A highway marker on State Route 447 approximately seven miles south of Nixon commemorates the battle.

Quinn River Camp No. 33 (Fort McDermit)
Humboldt County

By August 1865, the center of the soldiers' offensive shifted to north-central Nevada. Camp No. 33 was established on the Quinn River to direct operations, provide supplies, repair equipment, tend the wounded and hold prisoners. On 6 August, Lieutenant Colonel Charles McDermit and a group of soldiers were returning to the camp after scouting to the southeast. Near the campsite a carefully staged ambush took his life. Based on the selection of the ambush site and the fact that other officers were allowed to pass, this was clearly a well-planned assassination aimed at McDermit. After he fell, two others were wounded before the Indians fled.[263]

Camp No. 33 (later Fort McDermit) had been established not only as a military garrison, but also as an assembly and distribution point for Indians desiring to avoid conflict with the military. Prior to the murder of McDermit, several Indians suspected to be hostile had been observed taking special note of which soldiers were the officers and specifically which officer was the chief. A Warner Lake Shoshone called Captain John is credited with the murder of McDermit.[264] (*See* Battle Creek.)

Born 7 May 1820, in Cambria County, Pennsylvania, the young McDermit worked as a cabinet maker until he was twenty-six. In 1846, he enlisted in the 2nd Pennsylvania Volunteers and went to war across the Rio Grande in Mexico. He quickly rose to second lieutenant of Company D, 2nd Pennsylvania Volunteers and, in 1848, was made first lieutenant of the company. Following his release from service in Vera Cruz he moved to California to seek his fortune in the gold fields. There he fostered a series of enterprises while concurrently serving as a citizen soldier in several Indian campaigns. He was elected Sheriff of Siskiyou County and, in 1859, he was elected to the California Assembly. At the outbreak of the Civil War, he volunteered and was selected to command Company M, 2nd California Cavalry. In November 1861, he was promoted to major and sent to take command of the garrison at Fort Churchill. Promoted to lieutenant colonel, in the spring of 1865, he had earned the reputation as an excellent leader, a fair man

The McDermit family, l. to r:: Charles, LTC McDermit, Sadie, Hannah Davidson McDermit. This photo was taken before the birth of Elizabeth Maude.
Courtesy: Nevada Historical Society

in dealing with the peaceful Indians, and a tenacious foe in dealing with those wanting war. McDermit left a widow, Hannah Davidson McDermit, and three children: Charles, Sadie, and an eight-month old daughter born at Fort Churchill, Elizabeth Maude.[265]

Rabbit Hole Station
Pershing County

Rabbit Hole was a commonly used geographic reference point and eventually a station on the trail between the Humboldt River and Honey Lake. In March 1864, it became the first point of refuge for prospectors W.F. White and Frank Thompson after they were attacked by a band of Indians farther to the north. In the attack their partner, Dr H. Smeathman, was shot from ambush while the three were prospecting. Only wounded, Smeathman cried out in vain as his two companions fled. Within two months, another group of seven prospectors were set upon and four of them killed at nearby Disaster Peak.[266]

In response, Company D, 1st Nevada Cavalry, under Captain A.B. Wells, made its first expedition in the field. They camped at Rabbit Hole on the night of 23 June 1864. Wells' report states: "... arrived at Rabbit Hole Station, on the Humboldt and Susanville road at dark. Grass very poor, water scarce, and no wood."[267] Soldiers of Company D passed through Rabbit Hole at least two more times over the next two months.[268] Second Lieutenant John Littlefield passed through the area again on 5 August, "Found good hay for stock, but water bad."[269] Showing the flag seemed to quiet the area for the remainder of the year. In 1865, the Black Rock Desert and the entire Humboldt River drainage became the most dangerous area in the Great Basin. Rabbit Hole became a frequently used rally point for both Indian groups and soldiers.

On 5 May 1865, James Emory was killed near here and another in the same party, a Mr. Spencer, was wounded. Emory and Spencer were part of a group of seven prospectors on their way to the Pine Forest Mining District to the northeast. The prospectors reported killing four of the Indians. This was one of several incidents in the Black Rock Desert-Paradise Valley area that foreshadowed the campaign that would close general hostilities in the Nevada.

From the Sulphur siding (on Nevada State Route 49 between Winnemucca and Gerlach) take the gravel road straight south approximately nine miles to Rabbit Hole. This site is remote and should only be visited in good weather.

Ragtown
Churchill County

Ragtown was the western destination of those crossing the Forty Mile Desert. So named for the 49'ers common practice of hanging freshly washed clothes among the trees and bushes while their livestock grazed and recovered from the crossing. It was a common meeting point for military units and others in the region. Ragtown is eight miles west of Fallon on US 50.

Redskin, 'Fort'
Humboldt County

The name was given by Lieutenant Colonel Charles McDermit after viewing the rock fortifications used by the Indians to defeat First Lieutenant John Littlefield, Company D, 1st Nevada Cavalry. Littlefield's withdrawal occurred on 7 May 1865, when he came upon a well-armed Indian force somewhere between Paradise Valley and the Tuscarora Range. The exact location is unknown.[270]

Reeds's Station
(*See* Camp Hays.)

Reese River Station (Jacobsville)
Lander County

This site was used by both the Pony Express and Overland Stage. a major commercial center in the early 1860s, the town peaked at nearly four hundred residents. Jacobsville included a telegraph relay station, a post office, three stores, and two hotels. After discovery of rich mineral deposits and development of Austin most of the occupants moved there. Rock foundations mark the location of the Overland facilities and other buildings. The original wooden Pony Express Station was burned by Indians in the summer of 1860. Nothing remains of the adobe buildings that were built to replace the destroyed wood structures. The site is on the west side of the Reese River just north of where it runs under US 50 approximately eight miles west of Austin, Nevada.[271]

Nevada Historical Marker 66 provides additional information near the site on US 50.

Riley, 'Fort'
Storey County

In May 1860, when word of Major Ormsby's defeat at Pyramid Lake reached Virginia City, the result was near panic. Concerned that the Indians' success would give them the confidence to attack the towns, citizens developed plans for their defense. While others fought the second battle of Pyramid Lake, women and children were moved within the stone walls of a partially completed Virginia Hotel, then under construction in Virginia City. The property was owned by business man Peter O'Riley and thus the name 'Fort' Riley. O'Riley and Patrick McLaughlin are credited with the original discovery of the Ophir Mines near Washoe Lake which were later developed by the more famous Henry Comstock.[272] The site is within Virginia City.

Roberts Creek Station
Eureka County

Originally called She-o-wi-te Creek (also 'Sheawit Creek') by Captain James Hervey Simpson, U.S. Topographical Engineers, in 1859, the creek was renamed in honor of Bolivar Roberts, western agent for the Pony Express. The first station was built in the spring of 1860. Within a few months the stock was run off and the station destroyed by Indians. It was rebuilt in June 1860, and served the Pony Express through its end and then the Overland Mail and telegraph until it was abandoned in 1869.

From Eureka, travel thirteen miles west on US 50 to Roberts Creek Road. On Roberts Creek Road go north-northwest fifteen miles to Roberts Creek Ranch. The station site is on private ranch land. Nothing remains of the early station.[273]

Ruby Valley Station, Camp at
White Pine County

The Ruby Valley Station was established as a mail station in 1859. The log cabins were mapped by Captain J.H. Simpson in his 1859 survey. Early in 1860, a log Pony Express Station was added to the collection of cabins. On 10 June, following the battles at Pyramid Lake, soldiers of Company B, 4th U.S. Artillery, from Camp Floyd, Utah, established a temporary camp adjacent to the small community of log buildings. Dispatched to Ruby Valley to protect travelers on the Overland Trail during the Indian troubles of the time, the soldiers were under the command of First Lieutenants Delavan Duane Perkins and Stephen H. Weed (*see* Egan Station). Their area of operations extended from Robert's Creek Station to the west to Deep Creek Station just east of the (future) Utah-Nevada boundary. The assignment was short lived and this temporary camp was abandoned by 9 October 1860. The site was used occasionally by troopers of the 1st U.S. Dragoons dispatched from the newly established Fort Churchill.

On 20 October 1861, First Lieutenant Eugene Mortimer Baker, Company A, 1st U.S. Dragoons, met with local Indians following an increase in depredations in the area. The Indians stated they wanted no trouble with the whites, but they had no food for the coming winter. Their usual supply of pine nuts, grass seeds and small game for the winter were not available. There were no pine nuts that year and the Overland Stage Company and travelers on the road had harvested all of the grass for their own use. Concurring in their plight, Baker reported, "If any outbreak occurs it will be because they are driven to it by starvation."[274]

The next month, Shoshone Chief Sho-kup died of consumption at the home of settler Charles Stebbins. When the Shoshones wanted to kill the chief's squaw, as was the custom, Stebbins refused to allow it. Through careful negotiations by militia Colonel Warren Wasson order was maintained.[275] The shortage of food without prospects of relief created tension between the tribes as well as with the white settlers. Within a few weeks, a Bannock chief under the care of a Shoshone medicine man died. As a result, the Bannocks killed the medicine man. This initiated sporadic fighting between the two tribes. Also, each tribe raided the whites and tried to blame the other, hoping the whites would retaliate. On 18 December 1861, Captain Edwin A. Rowe, Company A, 2nd California Cavalry, reported his assessment and actions stating,

"I started the twenty-five men and two teams (under the charge of Captain [Daniel] McLean and Lieutenant [William H.] Chipman, [both of Company H] numbering in the aggregate twenty-nine), on the morning of the 17th instant ... I furnished them thirty days' rations. The Over-land Mail Company have agreed with Governor Nye to furnish forage, as they have particularly asked for the force to be sent. I desire to have the views of the general and the department in relation to this matter, as it may be necessary to forward more supplies in case the command remains there any length of time ... .

Rowe also stated his expectation that Governor Nye would soon be sending provisions for the Indians in the area.[276] Supplies were distributed and trouble was avoided through the winter months.

Under the protection of the military, the Camp and settlement at Ruby Valley prospered. Located on the Overland Trail traders provided services and a convenient rest along the way. It became a focal point for Indians, prospectors, travelers and settlers in what was then western Utah Territory. In April 1862, the Ruby Valley Post Office was established. In July 1862, the 2nd California Cavalry, under Colonel Patrick Edward Connor, used the Ruby Valley as one of their camp sites en route to their permanent assignment at Fort Douglas, Utah.[277] In November 1862, the military component was moved to more permanent quarters a few miles to the north. (*See* Fort Ruby.) A boundary change eventually put the area in Nevada Territory.

above: Officers' Quarters at Fort Ruby.
Courtesy: University of Nevada-Reno Library
below: Marker at Fort Ruby site.
Courtesy: The Author

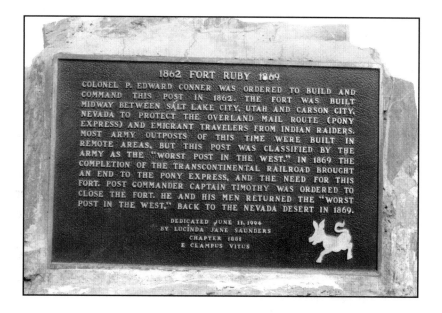

1862 FORT RUBY 1869
COLONEL P. EDWARD CONNER WAS ORDERED TO BUILD AND
COMMAND THIS POST IN 1862. THE FORT WAS BUILT
MIDWAY BETWEEN SALT LAKE CITY, UTAH AND CARSON CITY,
NEVADA TO PROTECT THE OVERLAND MAIL ROUTE (PONY
EXPRESS) AND EMIGRANT TRAVELERS FROM INDIAN RAIDERS.
MOST ARMY OUTPOSTS OF THIS TIME WERE BUILT IN
REMOTE AREAS, BUT THIS POST WAS CLASSIFIED BY THE
ARMY AS THE "WORST POST IN THE WEST." IN 1869 THE
COMPLETION OF THE TRANSCONTINENTAL RAILROAD BROUGHT
AN END TO THE PONY EXPRESS, AND THE NEED FOR THIS
FORT. POST COMMANDER CAPTAIN TIMOTHY WAS ORDERED TO
CLOSE THE FORT. HE AND HIS MEN RETURNED THE "WORST
POST IN THE WEST," BACK TO THE NEVADA DESERT IN 1869.

DEDICATED JUNE 11, 1994
BY LUCINDA JANE SAUNDERS
CHAPTER 1881
E CLAMPUS VITUS

The most likely site of the early military camp is in close proximity to the Ruby Valley Pony Express station on the Overland Trail. The station is on private land and is marked with a rock monument and brass plate commemorating the Pony Express route. The old log Pony Express station itself has been relocated to the museum in Elko. It represents an excellent example of many of the log structures used during early settlement of the Great Basin.[278]

Ruby, Fort
White Pine County

After establishing a military presence, beginning in 1860, and a semi-permanent camp in 1861, troubles continued. In August 1862, eleven emigrants were killed by Indians on the Humboldt River to the north. (*See* Gravelly Ford.) Depredations throughout the area increased. The Overland Stage reported the loss of one hundred and fifty horses, seven stations burned, and sixteen men killed.[279] Operating out of the camp in Ruby Valley, Companies H and K, 2nd California Cavalry, were involved in various skirmishes along the Humboldt River in the fall of 1862.[280] The need for a permanent garrison in Ruby Valley was soon recognized. In September 1862, Brigadier General George Wright, commanding the Department of the Pacific, issued the order to establish such a post at the south end of the Ruby Mountains.[281] By November 1862, Major Patrick A. Gallagher with two companies of the 3rd California Infantry had constructed an adobe and log post a few miles north of the original camp.[282] Designated Fort Ruby, its mission was to protect commerce along the Overland and Emigrant Trails. In a report prepared on 22 November 1862, Gallagher reported the theft of ten horses, one mule, and one beef in the vicinity of the post.[283] The winter of 1862-63 was harsh and native food sources were depleted. On 2 April 1863, Gallagher reported that many Indian had camped near Fort Ruby and were seeking handouts and relief through the winter months.[284]

Farther to the southeast, hostilities along the Nevada-Utah border increased significantly in the spring of 1863. Soldiers from

Fort Ruby were placed at all of the Overland stations on either side of the post. In May 1863, Captain S.P. Smith with Company K, 2nd California Cavalry, led an expedition from Fort Ruby into Steptoe Valley (*See* Duck Creek, Schell Creek Station and Spring Valley). The expedition involved several skirmishes and was successful in that it restored order and led to a treaty with the Goshute Indians in June 1863.[285]

On 1 October 1863, an accord, known as the Treaty of Ruby Marsh, was signed with the Western Shoshone. In essence, the Shoshone agreed not to molest whites in their area, to allow white development and settlement, and to eventually occupy reservations. In exchange they would receive $5000 in goods per year for twenty years. The treaty was signed by Governor James W. Nye of Nevada, Governor James Duane Doty of Utah, and twelve Shoshone Chiefs. Lieutenant Colonel J.B. Moore, 3rd California Infantry, and Jacob T. Lockhart, Indian Agent, also signed as witnesses.[286] Although the treaty was not ratified until 26 June 1866, it significantly reduced hostilities with most Indians in eastern Nevada.

The California military companies at Fort Ruby continued their service there until mid-1864. On 28 July 1864, troops from Company B, 1st Nevada Infantry, under Captain George Alva Thurston relieved them. The mission of the post remained the same: to guard the Overland Route from Austin to the Utah border and the Emigrant Trail north to the headwaters of the Humboldt River.[287]

With natural food supplies depleted, depredations increased significantly early in the winter of 1864. In correspondence of 21 December 1864, Thurston reported, "There are Indians at all of the stations between Ruby and Austin, and a great many in the vicinity of the latter place, all destitute of food and clothing."[288] Thurston urged some form of relief through distribution of food and clothing. "I believe if we make good our part of the treaty they also will do the same."[289] Efforts were made and the distribution of food occurred.

During the spring and summer of 1865, soldiers from Fort Ruby participated in the campaign centered around Paradise Valley. This campaign essentially ended organized Indian fighting in northern Nevada. In December 1865, regular U.S. Army troops began replacing volunteer units in the West. On 1 January 1867 Fort Ruby was officially redesignated as a Camp.[290] Completion of the transcontinental railroad along the northern end of the Ruby Mountains changed the patterns of commerce. Travel on the Overland Trail diminished significantly. On 10 March 1869, the decision was made to abandon the post and move the garrison to Camp Halleck approximately sixty miles to the north. On 20 September 1869, the last troops left Camp Ruby.[291]

Captain Thurston was one of many of the Nevada cavalry and infantry officers that were accepted for service in regular U.S. Army units. In December 1865, he mustered out of Company B, 1st Nevada Infantry, and by March 1867, was approved for a commission as a second lieutenant in 4th U.S. Cavalry. He was promoted to first lieutenant in 1868 and transferred to the 3rd U.S. Artillery in 1874. He was promoted to captain in December 1889 and died in July 1892.

Drive either thirty miles west from Ely or 47 miles east from Eureka on US 50 to the paved road on the north side of the highway. Note your speedometer reading and take this side road toward the north. In about two miles the road forks; take the left (west) fork and continue traveling in a northerly direction. Eventually, the paved surface turns to a graded gravel road. Avoid side roads and continue north-northwest, gradually crossing the floor to the west side of Long Valley. The road will take you through a wooded pass and on toward the prominent mountain range to the north. The site of Fort Ruby is approximately fifty-two miles from US 50 on the flatland on the southeast toe of the Ruby Mountains. Look for several cottonwood trees around a small pond. There is a stone monument with a brass plate commemorating the site. There are also several abandoned trailer houses and the burned ruin of a modern house. Only the small stone building by the pond dates back to the time of the post. The trip is worthwhile for the stark scenery, the solitude, and the remote sense of interior Nevada. However, the trash and debris of more recent habitation at this important site in Nevada's history can be a disappointment if not forewarned. The site is on private land.

Saint Mary's Station
Pershing County

A detachment of twenty-seven soldiers of Company D, 1st Nevada Cavalry, used the vicinity of the station and hotel as a camp 30 July to 4 August 1864. Ordered to investigate rumors of Indian and Confederate trouble at Unionville, Second Lieu-tenant John Littlefield left his detachment at Saint Mary's Station while he rode alone to Unionville. On 2 August, he rejoined the detachment and began the trip back to Smoke Creek Station.[292] The site was commonly used as a meeting place and crossing on the Humboldt River. It is named for the privately established Saint Mary's Hotel on the north bank of the Humboldt River.

The site is about one half mile upstream from the high water of present-day Rye Patch Reservoir.[293] From Exit 145 (Imlay) on I-80 take the improved road to the west approximately four and one quarter miles. The hotel site is on the bluff. Nothing remains of the structure.

Sand Springs Station
Churchill County

Often menaced during the Indian Wars, the roofless rock facility here served both the Overland Stage and the Pony Express. It also served as a resting spot for soldiers en route between Forts Churchill and Ruby. Poor water and constantly drifting fine sand were the greatest problems at the site. Two sets of rock structures are found here and the sequence of their use is unknown.

Travel east approximately twenty-five miles on US 50 from Fallon, Nevada. BLM and State of Nevada signs mark the route to the southern site. The first set of rock structures is a short distance north of the US highway and several hundred yards west of the access road to the sand dunes. The second site is approximately one and one half miles northwest of the first, and more obvious, rock site mentioned above.[294]

Schell Creek Station (Fort Schellbourne and Camp Schell)
White Pine County

Originally built to support Chorpenning's mail service in 1860, the Schell Creek Station was the scene of much action. On 16 July 1860, following their defeat at Egan Station, a group of Goshute Indians killed the three employees here. They burned the station and then drove off the livestock.[295] During the spring of 1863, several attacks along the Overland Trail led the military to keep soldiers at each of the stations on the trail. In late March 1863, the stagecoach was ambushed by Indians a few miles east of the station. Five soldiers riding the stage returned fire and the only known loss in the encounter was one horse in the stage's team. Such incidents became more common and, in early May 1863, soldiers from Company E, 3rd California Infantry, were assigned to protect the station.[296] On 2 May, Captain Samuel P. Smith with Company K, 2nd California Cavalry, camped at the Schell Creek Station during the campaign into Steptoe and Spring Creek Valleys.[297] (*See* Duck Creek.) Although never carried on official records as a fort, the frequent presence of soldiers earned it the name Fort Schellbourne.[298]

Schell Creek Station is about forty-five miles north of Ely on US Highway 93, three and one half miles east of Schellbourne, Nevada. The site is privately owned and occupied by several old buildings, some of which probably existed in the 1860s. The interpretive display at Schellbourne provides information about the Pony Express and other area history.

Scott, Camp
Humboldt County

In July 1866, Major General Henry W. Halleck issued the order to establish a post in Paradise Valley. A site was selected a few miles north of the town of Paradise Valley and on 12 December 1866, Captain Murray Davis arrived with troops from Company A, 8th U.S. Cavalry.[299] Within a few weeks Second Lieutenant John Lafferty, a veteran of Indian fighting as a Captain with the California Cavalry, was in the field with soldiers from the post. On 17 January 1867, riding from Camp Scott he engaged a group of Indians near the headwaters of the Little Humboldt. He succeeded in killing two of the party and destroyed their camp and supplies.[300] The following month, on 15 February, he successfully engaged another group on Black Slate Mountain. Returning to the field, on 20 February, he pursued another band on the south fork of the Little Humboldt, but they escaped into the mountains in a heavy snow.[301] In late March, with fourteen soldiers, he was again tracking and chasing a band of Indians through a heavy snow storm. On the ninth day of the chase (23 March 1867) he overtook them, killing six and destroying their arms and camp.[302]

By the summer of 1867, Lafferty's diligent pursuit of all hostile Indians in the proximity of the post seemed to have made the area relatively safe for the inhabitants of Paradise Valley. However, on 1 August, while on a fishing excursion with Lafferty, James A. Banks, Speaker of the House in the Nevada Legislature, was killed within a few miles of the camp. Lafferty and a second visitor, a Reverend Temple from New York, had been slowly fishing their way downstream along Cottonwood Creek ahead of Banks. Lafferty noticed that Banks had not caught up to them so he went back up stream to look for him. On the side of the stream he found the thirty-nine year old Banks, shot with an arrow in the breast and stripped of his clothes. After the funeral it was learned that three Indians from a larger group of renegades were responsible for the death. The first attempt to locate them failed; however, in the second attempt Lafferty tracked the group to a site near the head waters of the South Fork of the Owyhee River. In the following battle, his command killed four Indians and captured four more. Later that same day, while scouting alone, Lafferty encountered four more Indians and in fierce fighting killed two more and took the other two as prisoners.[303] Over the next few months he continued his relentless campaign against renegade Indians in the hills and mountains around Paradise Valley.

Lafferty's daring and success frequently appeared in the newspapers. He had a level of notoriety and a prominent profile not necessarily consistent with his station as a subordinate lieutenant at this remote post. Lafferty enjoyed a well-earned reputation as a popular, aggressive, and capable officer in the field and had nothing to prove.

In November, First Lieutenant Joseph Karge took command of Camp Scott. Karge had emigrated to the United States from

Germany before the Civil War. He had served as a lieutenant colonel in the 1st New Jersey Cavalry, attained the rank of colonel in the 2nd New Jersey Cavalry and had been breveted to brigadier general in 1865. Now, reduced to first lieutenant he was in command of a detachment of cavalry in one of the most isolated posts of the U.S. Army.[304] Lafferty had been in the area for several years, had considerable experience and possessed skill as an Indian fighter not held by Karge. On the other hand, Karge planned a military career and soon found the reputation he obtained during the Civil War in the east meant little in this new setting. He had to quickly make a new mark if he was to succeed. On 19 November, Karge's first attempt at Indian fighting failed to produce any results. The seeds of a clash with Lafferty were clearly present.[305]

The winter of 1867-68 was particularly harsh. A group of about twenty Indians, under the renowned renegade leader Big Foot, ran off all of the stock from M.W. Haviland's ranch in the valley. On 29 April 1868, Karge ordered newly arrived Second Lieutenant Pendleton Hunter, Sergeant John Kelley, Corporal Thomas Reed, and Private Thomas Ward to pursue Big Foot and his band. A civilian named John Rogers accompanied the patrol in the hopes of finding a horse he had lost earlier. Most of the soldiers in Hunter's group were new to the area and only Kelley had experience in Indian fighting.

Both Karge and Lafferty were now First Lieutenants, with Karge in command. Lafferty had accepted his subordinate role, but nothing happened through the winter months to improve the relationship between the two men. Upon hearing of Hunter's mission Lafferty was livid. Concerned for Hunter and unable to keep his thoughts to himself Lafferty assailed Karge, calling his decision to send Hunter into the field "committing murder." Conflict between the two erupted into a heated exchange. However, given the stakes, Lafferty was able to gain approval to mount a patrol to go after the green second lieutenant. Hunter tracked the Indian band to Deep Canyon, only eight miles from the post. In his naive haste to apprehend Big Foot, Hunter blindly led his men into an ambush. Almost immediately Kelley and Ward were mortally wounded. The horses were soon lost and Hunter was badly wounded. Now dismounted, Reed was the only one capable of defending their position. Rodgers ran on foot toward the post for help. His flight was successful and a rescue party was quickly organized at Camp Scott. Both the rescuers and Lafferty's patrol reached Hunter's beleaguered party at the same time. Confronted by the two mounted forces, Big Foot and his band withdrew and escaped into the mountains. Alone, Reed had held off the twenty Indian attackers until help arrived. For the valiant defense of his wounded comrades against the vastly superior odds Reed received an award (see note below).[306]

Hunter fully recovered from his wounds. On 1 January 1871, both he and Karge left the service from separate stations. After the Hunter incident, Lafferty was transferred to Arizona. In 1870, he receive a disabling wound during in a fight with Apache Indians in the Chiricahua Mountains. While attempting to retrieve the bodies of fallen comrades an Apache bullet carried away a portion of his lower jaw disabling him for life. He lived with his wound for nearly thirty years before dying of natural causes on 15 October 1899.[307]

A Corporal James Reed, Company A, 8th U.S. Cavalry, received the Medal of Honor for "defending his position against 17 Indians in Arizona on 29 April 1868." Records show that on that date, Company A, 8th U.S. Cavalry, had not yet been assigned to Arizona and was still assigned to Camp Scott in Nevada. In addition, Company A is reported as having been involved in an engagement near Camp Scott in Nevada on 29 April 1868. There is no record of any military engagement by any unit in Arizona on that date. There is every reason to believe the Medal of Honor was presented to Corporal Thomas Reed for remaining behind to save the life of Lieutenant Hunter in Deep Canyon near Camp Scott, Nevada. In all likelihood paperwork on the award did not catch up to Reed until both he and the unit had been reassigned to Arizona. If this is correct this is the only award for valor presented to any soldier for hostile action in the State of Nevada.[308]

On 19 February 1871, Camp Scott was ordered abandoned as no longer being necessary.[309] The site is on private land approximately four miles north-northwest of Paradise Valley. The officer's quarters are currently used as a residence. Other remaining buildings have been incorporated into the ranch operation headquartered on the site. Special care should be taken to respect the privacy of the owners of this property.

Silver City Fortifications
Lyon County

Temporary fortifications were constructed in the vicinity of Silver City following the defeat of William Ormsby at Pyramid Lake on 12 May 1860. Nothing remains of these fortifications.[310]

Silver Creek, Camp on
Lander County

In the spring of 1865, Indian hostilities in central Nevada were increasing daily. First Lieutenant W.G. Seamonds and Second Lieutenant John U. Tolles, with forty soldiers from Company B, 1st Nevada Infantry, and ten friendly Indians, as well as an artillery piece, were dispatched from Fort Ruby to Austin to provide security in the area. Referred to as Camp No. 7 in official reports, this site was used from 20 May to 6 June 1865. From this camp, Seamonds obtained additional horses and the report states he, "here divided the command, himself taking the twenty mounted men, the Indians, and the artillery piece, and marching with Lieutenant Colonel McDermit, 2nd California Cavalry, to the recent battlefield of Captain Wells against the Pi-Ute and Bannock Indians."[311] (*See* Tuscarora Range.) Tolles was left in command of the remaining infantrymen.

On the journey north up the Reese River, Seamonds had an opportunity to use the mountain howitzer. In the northern reaches of the river an Indian party was encountered in the hills to the west. A few shots were fired from the howitzer into the Indian group. With no losses to the soldiers and unknown losses to the Indians the soldiers continued up the river valley.

After Seamonds left for the expedition to the north, a group of three Indians were observed about two miles from the camp stealing cattle belonging to a Mr. Worthington. Tolles and fifteen soldiers immediately gave chase on foot from the camp. The

Indians, two of them mounted and one on foot, were driving eight to ten head of cattle east up Silver Creek. The Indians were slowed by the rough terrain, thus Tolles' troops were able to get within musket range. They fired several shots, but to no avail. The Indians cleared the crest with the livestock escaping over the mountains to Grass Valley.

In a situation best appreciated by military veterans, this relatively minor incident is carried as an 'engagement' in the Official Records. However, engagements of far greater consequence are missing in these same records. They are often left instead to the obscure text on the back page of some now defunct newspaper of the time. It appears that even in 1865 the deeds of soldiers with an ample supply of ink, paper, and the free time to write often found a place in recorded history while the greater deeds of soldiers more heavily engaged go unrecorded and, thus, unnoticed today. Accounts of the fight at Table Mountain (*see* Tuscarora Range) in which two soldiers were killed, four wounded and, the command withdrew under overwhelming Indian fire is not in the Official Records. This is not to belittle the deeds of Tolles' detachment, but rather to lament the loss of history due to the lack of a scribe. This irony is particularly apparent in the Indian Wars where most engagements involved Army units smaller than company size; often led by captains, lieutenants, and sergeants. The same is even more true for the individual and collective heroism of the Indian warriors.

Silver Creek drains from the east into the Reese River approximately sixteen miles north of Austin on State Route 305.

Simpson Park Station
Lander County

Built in early April 1860, the original station was destroyed a little over a month later during the Indian trouble the following May. Station keeper James Alcott was killed and the stock taken. Soldiers were requested, but priority initially went to assigning them in the vicinity of more populated areas. Bolivar Roberts, division manger, hired his own guards until soldiers from Camp Floyd,

Utah, began patrolling the route. Prior to the establishment of Austin, this station contained a blacksmith shop and served as a principle stop for commerce and emigrants using the trail. The area had a cemetery which was reported to contain several graves.

In 1862, various units of the 2nd California Cavalry and 3rd California Infantry camped near here en route to their permanent assignments during the Civil War at Camp Douglas, Utah, and beyond. On 19 October 1863, Captain Noyes Baldwin, with the Companies A and B, 1st Nevada Cavalry, camped overnight here also en route to Camp Douglas, Utah.[312]

The site is located on private land in the mouth of Simpson Canyon on the east side of the Toiyabe Range. From Austin go thirteen miles east on US 50 to a gravel road. Go north approximately six miles. This is private land and permission should be obtained to view the site. Beyond the rock outline of the station foundation nothing remains of either the facilities or the cemetery.[313]

Camp No. 16
Humboldt County

Camp No. 16 was Lieutenant Colonel Charles McDermit's field headquarters and base camp for the largest maneuver of the Indian War in Nevada. It was established on 30 June 1865, at the northern base of the mountain range that divides the drainages of the Humboldt and Owyhee Rivers. The number '16' has no special significance other than it was the sixteenth camp site used by McDermit's party after leaving Austin in May. From this camp McDermit assigned a sector for each of the units at his disposal to "protect settlers and punish marauding Indians" and otherwise disrupt any coalition of renegade Bannocks, Paiutes, and Shoshones that may have formed in the area.

Major Michael O'Brien, 6th California Infantry, was ordered to report to Camp No. 16 from Fort Churchill to take command of the base camp and oversee operation of the headquarters for the campaign. Captain James T. Hill, took Company D, 6th California Infantry, to protect settlers and commerce along the Quinn River to the west. First Lieutenant Richard A. Osmer, with Company B,

2nd California Cavalry, was assigned a similar mission in the area between the Humboldt and Reese Rivers. Captain J.C. Doughty, with Company I, 2nd California Cavalry, was sent to Gravelly Ford to coordinate operations in that area with Company B, 1st Nevada Infantry, from Camp Ruby. Captain Almond B. Wells with Company D and Lieutenant John Littlefield with Company E, both 1st Nevada Cavalry, as well as Captain William Wallace with Company A, 1st Nevada Infantry, accompanied McDermit across the range of mountains between the Humboldt and Owyhee Rivers; thence east to the head of the Humboldt River. Lieutenant William G. Seamonds, with twenty mounted men from Company B, 1st Nevada Infantry, was attached to accompany Captain Doughty to Gravelly Ford. Captain Robert C. Payne of Company E, 1st Nevada Cavalry, was put in charge of the supplies and field trains to be centrally located at Camp No. 14 twenty-five miles to the south. Thus ordered, each unit moved from Camp No. 16 to carry out its assignment.[314]

The exact location of Camp No. 16 is unknown. Based on extrapolation of movements from various known points in the record, it is most likely in the vicinity of Mahogany Pass in the Calico Mountains approximately twenty-four air miles north-northwest of Paradise Valley. This Camp 16 should not be confused with other 'camp 16s' found in the reports of the time. The lack of standard geographic names generated the practice of sequentially numbering the campsites of an expedition. For example, Captain Wells reports his bivouac at "camp no. 16" on the night of 24 August 1864, on his journey from Susanville, California, back to Fort Churchill. This is clearly not the same camp as McDermit's July 1865 camp, but rather the result of both officers sequentially numbering the camp sites of their separate expeditions.

Smith Creek Station
Lander County
This was the first station in Shoshone country on the traditional boundary between the Paiute and Shoshone Indians. It was an overnight stop for Warren Wasson while en route to parlay

with Shoshones over the death of the friendly Chief Chokup. Named by Captain J.H. Simpson, U.S. Topographical Engineers, for one of his men, "Both the stream and the canyon I call after my assistant, Lieut. J.L. Kirby Smith."[315]

Smith Creek Station served travelers on the Overland Trail for many years. It was the site of many Indian raids. In addition, the station has the unusual distinction of being the site of the first legally tried capital crime in Nevada Territory. William Carr, a Pony Express Rider, murdered Bernard Chessy following an argument.[316] Carr was tried in the court of Judge John Cradlebaugh (later Adjutant General for Nevada), convicted and then hanged at Carson City in late 1860. This was the first such legal proceeding in the Territory.[317]

It is also the site of an earlier conflict in which Station Manager H. Trumbo was shot by rider Montgomery Maze. Trumbo had been harassing Maze by repeatedly pointing an empty pistol at him and snapping the trigger. After continuation of the treatment into the next day, Maze took his rifle and shot Trumbo above the hip. Fearing retaliation, Maze left the station, but not until he obtained signatures from witnesses stating that Trumbo had provoked the attack. This may be the earliest reported incident of workplace violence associated with mail delivery.

On 19 November 1861, the Pony Express and Overland Station were located at the summit of the Desatoya Mountains. The original site is on private land and local inquiry should be made before visiting. It is incorporated into the ranch buildings of the Smith Creek Ranch and lies fourteen miles north of Nevada State Route 2 between the Reese River and the Desatoya Mountains approximately thirty-three miles southwest of Austin, Nevada.[318]

Smoke Creek Station/Camp Smoke Creek
Washoe County

The site was first developed by T.T. Kingsbury as a stage station on Noble's cutoff in May 1857. Later William Kingsbury built a hotel and trading post at the site. In the spring of 1862, citizens of the Honey Lake area complained of increasing Indian

Guidons from Company D and I,
2nd California Cavalry, c. 1862.
Courtesy: Eastern California Museum

depredations. Captain George F. Price, commanding Company M, 2nd California Cavalry met with them in late May 1862. In their letter the citizens characterized the problem:

> ... this valley does not belong to any particular tribe, but was the common resort of the Pah-Utes, Shoshones, Modocs, Pitts, and Bannocks, and consequently the valley is subject to depredations of all these tribes, and it is very difficult to fasten the roguery where it belongs. One tribe will commit outrages and lay it to the others. Also, that there has never been an Indian agent in this valley [Honey Lake], and no attention paid to the most of the tribes who are in the valley who are in constant habit of molesting us; also that there are several portions of these different bands who are renegades from their tribes, and whose location is in the country east and north of us, watered by Smoke Creek, Willow Creek, and outlets from Eagle Lake. These renegades are subject to no treaties made with the heads of their different tribes, but are under control of petty chiefs who rove about the frontiers stealing stock and killing small parties of whites.[319]

Price's expedition validated the citizens' concerns and troops were first assigned to areas in California and then Nevada.

The camp at Smoke Creek, Nevada, was first established as a semi-permanent camp on 15 December 1862. Lieutenant Henry W. Williams and twenty-five soldiers of Company C, 2nd California Cavalry, were sent from Fort Crook, California. Their mission was to protect commerce on the Honey Lake-Humboldt River road. The camp contained crude quarters for the soldiers and stables for the horses.[320]

On 22 October 1863, Company D, 1st Nevada Cavalry, under First Lieutenant Daniel Firman from Fort Churchill relieved the California cavalry.[321] He was relieved by Lieutenant Oscar Jewett in December 1863. Company D, 1st Nevada Cavalry, was relieved by Company A, 1st Nevada Infantry, under Captain M.R. Hassett on 28 July 1864. Lieutenant John Littlefield Company D, 1st Nevada Cavalry, used the camp during the summer of 1864. On his detail from Honey Lake to Unionville he reported, "... arrived Smoke Creek Station at 10.30 a.m. Good water and hay for stock. Took in Government grain for horses, and purchased beef for men. Heavy showers of rain during the night. July 27, left Smoke Creek at 5 a.m. ..."[322] He camped there again on 7 August 1864 on his return trip.

On 10 July 1865, Captain W.L. Knight, 2nd California Cavalry, camped near quarters owned by Kingsbury & Company. These were the same quarters formerly occupied by troops previously stationed in the area. In his report Knight complained about conditions in the area:

> [The quarters] are only large enough to accommodate thirty-five men and the stable will accommodate thirty horses. They are not adequate for half my command, but when I get my men distributed along the road between here and Pueblo the quarters will accommodate what will remain here, if it is intended that I shall hire quarters. I have nothing but shelter-tents, and the winds blow so hard every afternoon that they are of but little use. There is not a tree or stick of timber fit for building purposes nearer than Susanville (that fifty miles). Sage brush is all the wood used here, or to be gotten for cooking purposes, nearer than about fifteen miles from here near the head of Smoke Creek, but before it can be gotten at considerable work will have to be done, making roads. I have several men sick, and there is no medicine here and no doctor nearer than Susanville.[323]

Knight's request to rent quarters was denied and most of his troops were then dispersed to stations along the trail to the east. Military use of the camp ended in April 1866. The camp and station take their name from the Smoke Creek Desert. This general area was first referred to by that name on an 1854 manuscript map for a proposed railroad route drawn by John A. Driebelis.[324]

The station is located in the northwestern corner of the Smoke Creek Desert. Go north from Gerlach nine miles on State Route 447; west on the maintained gravel road thirty-two and one half miles. Smoke Creek Station and locations referred to as Camp Smoke Creek are on private land on the west side of Smoke Creek.

Local tradition holds that the soldiers also camped frequently near the mouth of the canyon two or three miles downstream.

A trail marker established by Trails West, Inc., in 1973, on the county road also identifies the site as a segment of the 1852 Noble's Cutoff; the 1858 Lander Cutoff; and the Fort Kearny-South Pass-Honey Lake Wagon Road. Water for the camp and station was provided by Smoke Creek and forage came from the large meadow upstream from the site. The actual camp site varied depending on the size of the contingent and their needs for space. Robber's Roost, approximately four miles north on the county road, was occasionally used as an alternate temporary camp site for small detachments. The significance of the two white crosses on the west side of the creek is unknown.

Soldier Meadows, Camp
Humboldt County

The meadow and hot springs were first reported by Captain John C. Fremont as his camp site on 31 December 1843. Beginning in 1862, the site was used more frequently as a bivouac site and pasture for military horses. This minor post was comprised of stone buildings used as a magazine, quarters for officers, and separate quarters for enlisted soldiers. These were connected by a protected passage to a nearby stable, also made of stone. The post was established to protect wagon traffic from the south joining the Susanville, California-Owyhee, Idaho route.[325] Located twenty miles south of Summit Lake and Camp McGarry, it was a frequent stop-over and campsite for soldiers in the field from a variety of posts including McGarry, Churchill, and Bidwell. The buildings found there now were constructed by soldiers from Camp McGarry.[326]

Soldier Meadows Ranch is a private bed and breakfast guest ranch offering a variety of outdoor activities, but no vehicle services. Start in Gerlach with a full tank of gas. Go northeast on State Route 34. At approximately eleven miles take the right unpaved fork marked Soldier Meadows Ranch. Continue north approximately fifty-three miles to Soldier Meadows Ranch. This is an exciting trip and you are nearly guaranteed to see antelope, wild horses, and some of the most remote and stark scenery in Nevada. It is well worth the trip, but is an adventure definitely needing forethought and planning.

Spring Valley Station
White Pine County

An Overland Stage station and possibly a Pony Express Station, it was built sometime after October 1860 and used through 1869. One story tells of a Pony Express rider known as 'Uncle Nick' Wilson. When he stopped at the station to change horses and eat supper, two Indians crept up and stole the horses. With two boys tending the station he gave chase. Running after them with his pistol drawn, he rounded a tree and was met by an arrow. The arrow lodged in his forehead a couple of inches above his left eye. The Indians fled with the horses while the boys tended to Wilson. One of the boys succeeded in pulling the shaft off, but the stone arrowhead remained in his forehead. The boys placed him under a tree and covered him with a blanket to give him comfort in his last hours. The following day men from the next station came to bury him, however, it seemed they were early as he was not yet dead. The funeral was postponed while a doctor from Ruby Valley was summoned. The doctor deemed him a hopeless case, but removed the arrowhead anyway. A few days later Howard Egan went to the station and Wilson was still living. The doctor was called again, treatment was provided, and in a few weeks Wilson was back riding for the Pony Express.[327]

Not much is known of the station. The most likely location is on the south end of the Antelope Range somewhere along the Overland Trail, approximately halfway between the stations at Antelope Springs and Schell Creek.

Spring Valley
White Pine County

On 5 May 1863, after the two skirmishes on Duck Creek,

Captain Samuel P. Smith took Company K, 2nd California Cavalry, east over the Schell Creek Range into Spring Valley. Moving at night they arrived on the morning of the 6th. At daylight they located another camp of Goshute Indians and immediately charged. A swamp in the path of the charge delayed the attack and gave the Goshutes an unexpected opportunity to escape. Even with this advantage twenty-three Indians were killed. There were no losses reported by the military. From here the soldiers scouted the area back to Camp Ruby arriving there on 10 May. The report of the expedition lists fifty-two Goshutes killed and one trooper wounded. Throughout the summer and early fall Company K was involved in other engagements to the east in Utah.[328]

In September 1875, one of the last incidents involving military-Indian action occurred in and around Spring Valley. Two miners, A. J. Leathers and James Tollard, offered two Goshute Indians fifty dollars to guide them to mineral deposits the Indians claimed to know about. No minerals were found and the miners refused to pay. In the dispute, To-Ba, one of the two Indians, killed Tollard. Leathers escaped to the nearby A.C. Cleveland ranch. Hearing the story, Cleveland chased down an Indian he thought was responsible. With the stated intention of turning him over to authorities Cleveland started back toward his ranch. However, the Indian was "killed trying to escape." Concurrently, some of Cleveland's employees discovered a second Indian. When the Indian refused to surrender his firearms to the ranch hands, he was killed.

About the same time, large groups of Goshute Indians were gathering in the wooded areas surrounding the valley. The settlers became concerned that an uprising was imminent. In actuality, the Indians were assembling for the age-old practice of harvesting pinyon nuts. Without realizing the situation Governor L.R. Bradley telegraphed, on 6 September 1875, U.S. Army Major General John M. Schofield in San Francisco. Bradley stated,

> Information most authentic from Pioche, Eureka, and Spring Valley, all unite in demands for troops and arms. Am unable to furnish them. Dispatch just at hand signed by all

Commissioners of Lincoln County, says 300 Indians surround Patterson and Cave Valley, and all the Indians in eastern Nevada appear to be on the war-path, and ask for 200 guns and ammunition. Most reliable information from Cherry Creek assures me that I am not misinformed.[329]

Concurrently, militia Major John H. Dennis, Quartermaster for the 2nd Brigade, Nevada militia, was ordered to assemble a force from the Eureka and Ruby Hill Guards (also militia units). Once assembled, they were to move to the area to restore order. Upon arriving Dennis found several Indians—men, women and children—peacefully gathering pinyon nuts in the woodlands. Among them was To-Ba. Upon request they surrendered him to Dennis. Local citizens then took custody of To-Ba and summarily hanged him for the murder of Tollard.[330] There is no record of any penalty for the killing of the other two innocent Indians. State Route 893 runs the entire length of Spring Valley.

Star City
Pershing County

Star City was a population center and mining town in the north end of the Humboldt Range. Although Unionville was the county seat for Humboldt County, Star City, a few miles to the north was the population center. In the early 1860s, both Unionville and Star City mustered militia cavalry companies. Known as the Buena Vista Guards, Cavalry (Unionville) and the Humboldt Rangers (Star City) their rolls contained approximately 250 names in September 1862. However, close examination of the rolls shows many of the same names in both companies. The companies never trained or received arms or equipment. Like many militia units the two companies were more a patriotic concept than a genuine force. The first real military presence came in mid-June 1864, when Captain A.B. Wells with Company D, 1st Nevada Cavalry, used Star City as a temporary camp.[331]

Following the burning of the Granite Creek Station in the spring of 1865, E.F. Dunne, a Notary Public in Star City, requested weapons and military assistance for the area. Dunne was on the 1862 muster rolls of the Humboldt Rangers and Adjutant General John Cradlebaugh mistakenly thought Dunne was an officer. Weapons were sent to Dunne and First Lieutenant Joel Wolverton, with a forty-seven man detachment from Company D, 1st Nevada Cavalry, was sent through Star City en route to Paradise Valley.[332] On 4 April 1865, Dunne forwarded a message to Fort Churchill that Wolverton had killed five Shoshones; sent twenty men to Paradise Valley and confirmed the massacre of civilians there. Wolverton's message requested more troops for Paradise Valley. He gave his location as being on the Humboldt River, forty-five miles northeast of Star City. Thirty armed citizens went to Paradise Valley, fifteen more to Granite Creek with more going the next day.[333]

A major offensive campaign by the military that summer and fall brought order to the area. (*See* Camp No. 16) In December 1865, with much of the nearby fighting over, Dunne was asked to return the weapons to the Adjutant General. His response is a quartermaster's classic nightmare:

> "In reply ... I think there is a mis-apprehension as to some points ... . Concerning charge 166 stand of arms to Humboldt County is, I think, correct, except they have been furnished on my demand as a private citizen, and not on a requisition of an officer of the company. For 100 stand I have receipted. Who receipted for the remaining 66 I do not know, as I did not receive or have the distribution of them. Concerning the disposition of the same they were immediately distributed to citizens, and have not been recalled. I made an effort to have our military company recognized by the department; drew petitions; wrote letters, etc. so as to have the guns received by a responsible organization, but I could get no reply from your office, and was preforce obliged to distribute guns indiscriminately where I supposed they would be most needed, and give greatest protection. Many have acted badly with the guns, taken them to Idaho without permission and failed to return or report them. On a call, many of the 166 stand issued here will NOT be forthcoming, 30% of them probably would be missing.
> Resp'y E.F. Dunne"[334]

Like the weapons, nothing exists of Star City today. Take exit 149 (Mill City) from I-80. Go approximately eleven miles south on State Route 400. Star City was in the foothills to the west in the Humboldt Range.

Storey, Fort
Washoe County
After the second battle at Pyramid Lake in 1860, the volunteer militia under Colonel John Hays and the U.S. regulars under Captain Joseph Stewart constructed earthworks for the defense of their position through the night. No attack came and on 4 June 1860 the command abandoned the site, moving farther south along the Truckee River. The earthwork fortifications were named for Captain Edward Faris Storey, commander of one of the two militia cavalry units used to screen ahead of the main body of soldiers during the second battle near Pyramid Lake. Storey had been at the forefront of the fighting and was shot through the lungs while in command of his unit.[335]

Nothing remains of the site, which is located along the Truckee River between Wadsworth and Nixon.[336]

Summit Lake, Camp
(*See* Camp McGarry.)

Sulphur Springs Station
Eureka County
Sulphur Springs Station first appears on an 1863 map of the Overland Stage and Mail Express route. It served the Overland Stage from 1861 to 1869. Not directly on the Pony Express route, the location was probably only used intermittently by the Pony Express when the Indian threat forced consolidation for defense.[337]

Take US 50 northeast from Eureka three miles to State Route 278. On State Route 278 continue north seventeen miles to Sadler-Brown Road. The site of the station is on private land approximately four miles north on Sadler-Brown Road.

Table Mountain Battle Site
(*See* Tuscarora Range.)

Trego Hot Springs
Pershing County

This was a temporary camp used by Company D, 1st Nevada Cavalry, intermittently in the summer of 1864. Captain A.B. Wells reported on 24 June 1864, "... arrived at Hot Springs Station [Trego Hot Springs], distance 20 miles directly west of Rabbit Hole, at 2 p.m.; wood and grass very scarce." On 5 August, Second Lieutenant John Littlefield also reported, "Stock in good condition; arrived Hot Springs 2 p.m.; distance 20 miles. Found hay and poor water."[338] The site is on the south edge of the Black Rock Desert approximately fourteen miles east of the junction of State Routes 447 and 48 (south of Gerlach).

Trinity, Fort
(*See* Eight Mile Station.)

Truckee River Bend
Washoe County

The area where the Truckee River bends to the north (near present-day Wadsworth) was a frequent meeting place during the Indian War. It was here that William Ormsby's force bivouacked the night before the disastrous defeat near Pyramid Lake on 12 May 1860. It was also here that Colonel Hayes and Captain Stewart assembled their forces before and after the second battle near Pyramid Lake a few weeks later in June.

On 23 May 1862, Governor Nye and Indian agent Warren Wasson met with Paiute Chief Old Winnemucca at the site. Wasson, a militia colonel, had long been an advocate of equitable treatment for the Indians. He respected their customs and honored their existing ties to particular tracts of land when white settlers first arrived in Nevada. The conference was arranged at Wasson's urging and had the simple objective of dialogue between the leaders of the whites and the Indians. The meeting was uneventful, but was a positive move in that it did establish the desired dialogue. The unfortunate aspect was that Governor Nye, while he could establish policies and take actions that favored peaceful relations with the Indians, had almost no control and only limited influence over the actions of the white population. Concurrently, Chief Winnemucca could attempt to influence other chiefs, but there were no lines of authority among the chiefs of the Indian population.[339]

In May 1865, the bend in the Truckee River was the site of another pivotal meeting in the relations between the Indians and the whites. Following up on complaints from the Pyramid Lake Paiutes, Lieutenant Colonel McDermit and his adjutant, Lieutenant Daniel Vanderhoff, discovered a new Indian Agent had leased grazing land belonging to the Indians without their concurrence. The agent was pocketing the money he received from white ranchers using the leased Indian land. In addition, $25,000 allocated for the benefit of the Indians had vanished without tangible results. Following a meeting on 7 May, the cattle were removed and the matter of the money was reported to the higher civilian and military authorities.[340] The site of these meetings is located on the Truckee River near present day Wadsworth.

Tuscarora Range (Table Mountain and Clover Valley)
Elko County

The spring of 1865 was the beginning of the most significant fighting in northern Nevada. The coalition and determination of the Indians was at its peak. Unaware of either the size or commitment of the Indian coalition, First Lieutenant John Little-field, Company D, 1st Nevada Cavalry, conducted a scouting mission east of Paradise Valley. On 7 May 1865, he encountered a large group of well-armed and fortified Indians. They had con-structed rock revetments and were clearly ready to engage Little-field's thirty-five man force. After initial contact he was forced to with-draw under withering fire. Sharply criticized in the newspapers for his decision to leave the field under fire, Littlefield was labeled a coward. A later visit to the site with Lieutenant Colonel McDermit and Captain Wells, in June, vindicated the lieutenant in the eyes of his commander and fellow officers. McDermit dubbed the battle site 'Fort Redskin' after the well-constructed rock fortifications built by the Indians.[341] The *Reese River Reveille* reported on 28 June,

> Many persons have done Lieutenant Littlefield great injustice by saying that he acted cowardly. His course was prudent, and he acted wisely in not rushing into a place where in all probability not one man in ten would have come out alive. Lieutenant Littlefield had only thirty-five men all told, and there were at least two hundred Indians well armed with rifles, and the deep canyon in which they were in was well defended on all sides by rifle pits so that they could load and shoot without being exposed to the fire of the soldiers. Lieutenant Seamonds says he was all over the ground and took a good look at it. There are at least twenty-five rifle pits, many large enough to hold thirty Indians, and the ground is situated so that the troops would have been compelled to dismount and attack, exposed in front to the breast works of the Indians.[342]

In spite of his fellow officers' affirmation, Littlefield would carry the stigma of cowardice until he clearly demonstrated his personal bravery in battle three months later in the Quinn River drainage. (*See* Willow Spring.)

After organizing a larger force, Captain A.B. Wells returned with Littlefield and sixty-six men of Company D. On 20 May, he encountered a large Indian force comprised of Paiutes, Bannocks, and Shoshone under Chief Zelauwick (also Zelanwick) in the Tuscarora Range. The Indians were well fortified in positions behind revetments constructed of rocks. They held the advantages of surprise, terrain, and numbers. The lowest estimate of their strength was five-hundred. At the time of the encounter, Wells' force had been depleted in that ten men were with the supply train and ten others were on a scout to a nearby area.

At approximately 3:00 p.m. Wells initiated his attack. Leaving a few men to attend the horses, he engaged the right flank with twenty men under Littlefield, while the remainder attacked on the left. The Indians remained concealed, holding their fire until the soldiers were within about seventy-five yards. After nearly four hours of repeated attempts to dislodge the Indian force and with darkness setting in, Wells sounded recall. Two of the Nevada cavalrymen, Privates Isaac Godfrey (twenty-seven years old from Canada) and James Munroe (nineteen years old from Illinois), were killed in the fighting. Godfrey was killed outright by a shot to the head. Munroe became isolated and was wounded in the torso and foot during the withdrawal. He died later in the hands of the Indians. Four other soldiers from the command were wounded.[343]

Unable to dislodge the Indians, and with night approaching, Captain Wells withdrew. The Indians pursued him. Under continuous harassing fire he established a defensive perimeter about two miles from the scene of the earlier fighting. During the night the Indians surrounded his force and prepared an ambush along his most likely route of escape. In the morning Wells sent an advanced party to scout the escape route. Within a short distance of the camp they were ambushed. Hearing the shots, Wells quickly organized the main body and moved toward the fighting. With his wounded in tow he quickly joined the advanced party. With the command reunited the soldiers successfully fought their way through the ambush to safety.[344]

This was the first major battle with a committed Indian force since Pyramid Lake in 1860. The Indians employed a well-coordinated defense which involved members of several tribes. They reacted quickly to Wells' withdrawal with a counterattack. They maintained contact and pressured Wells into a hasty defense. The following morning they executed a planned ambush of Wells' advanced party on the escape route, forcing Wells to abandon his defensive position and consolidate his forces to make good his escape. Many military supplies and weapons were lost. The battle clearly went to the Indians. Following the battle, some of the soldiers reported seeing whites among the Indian force. Whether these were Mormons, Confederate sympathizers disgruntled over the outcome of the Civil War, or merely lawless white renegades living among the Indians is unknown. However, the significance of this combination of factors was not lost on the leadership of the whites. (*See* Camp No. 16)

The exact site of the battle is not known. It has been reported as Clover Valley, Table Mountain, and Godfrey Peak (named for the Isaac Godfrey killed in the battle). No existing geographical reference matches the information in the records, but the site is most likely on the west face of the Tuscarora Range.

Unionville
Pershing County

Unionville was a mining town on the east slope of the Humboldt Range. As a population center, it provided a central point for military operations along the Humboldt River until Dun Glen proved more favorable.[345] It was originally named Buena Vista and then became known as Dixie. A vote on 4 July 1861, after the beginning of the Civil War, showed there were more northern sympathizers than southern and the name was changed to Unionville.[346]

Take exit 149 (Mill City) from I-80. Go approximately sixteen miles south on State Route 400 to a marked turn off to the west. Unionville is about three miles west in the Humboldt Range.

Vicksburg Mines
Humboldt County

On 7 February 1867, Lieutenant G.F. Foote, with soldiers from Company B, 1st U.S. Cavalry, and the 9th U.S. Infantry, engaged a group of Indians at the Vicksburg Mines, eleven miles south of the Nevada-Oregon border.[347] No details of the engagement are available other than the fact that one Indian was wounded. The Vicksburg Mines are on the west slope of the Pine Forest Range eleven miles southwest of Denio Junction.

Virginia City
Storey County

Indian problems in the Virginia City area were almost non-existent. However, the secessionist cause was far more evident. On 5 June 1861, the Confederate flag was raised at Virginia City by southern sympathizers. General Edwin A. Sumner, head of the U.S. Army Department of the Pacific, ordered Major George A.H. Blake, 1st U.S. Dragoons, to investigate the incident. Blake's follow up confirmed a small, but dedicated, faction in support of the

CAVALRY VOLUNTEERS
FOR ACTIVE SERVICE
IN UTAH AND NEW MEXICO.

WANTED, ONE HUNDRED ABLE-bodied men, to fill up Company D, First Battalion, N. T. V., to be mustered into the service of the United States for three years or during the war. Clothing and subsistence will be furnished immediately on being enrolled. Recruits to be armed, equipped, and mounted when the company organization is complete. Recruits desiring to furnish their own horses and horse equipments will be allowed forty cents per day extra. The organization of a company of mounted troops consists of eight sergeants, eight corporals, two blacksmiths, two buglers, one saddler, one wagoner, and eighty privates. One hundred dollars bounty is guaranteed by the laws of the United States in addition to the regular pay.

Recruiting offices are opened at the following places:

Blue Wing Saloon, one door north of the Post-office, Gold Hill.

Overland Saloon, Dayton.

Grass Valley Saloon, No. 3 south B street, Virginia.
MILO GEORGE,

and tf Capt. Co. D, First Battalion N. T. V.

southern cause. He ordered his Quartermaster, Captain T. Moore, to Virginia City to collect any arms and ammunition from the sympathizers. Moore's report states,

> On my arrival at Virginia everything was comparatively quiet, although there was considerable excitement among the advocates of the Southern rebellion. Immediate examination of all buildings suspected of containing arms was made. The building on which the rebel flag was hoisted a few days since was found to contain no arms, and the proprietor assured me that the flag was hoisted more for a joke than with the intention of causing any excitement. His statement, I believe was intended for a blind, as I was subsequently informed from the most reliable residents of the place that there was, beyond a doubt, an organization to subvert the authority of the Federal Government in this Territory and declare in favor of the Confederate States.[348]

There is no doubt that a Confederate organization existed within the area. The majority of the residents favored the Union cause, thus forcing the southerners to generally remain in the shadows. Secessionists organized a clandestine group known as the 'Order of the Golden Circle.' There being few real secrets in Virginia City, a counter group called the 'Union League' was soon formed.[349] As the Confederate army suffered defeat in the east, sympathizers in California and Nevada hoped to move the cause to the west. In September 1864, Major Milo George, with soldiers from Companies D and E, 1st Nevada Cavalry, went briefly to Virginia City to investigate new rumors of a secessionist uprising and to 'show the flag.' Although a small group of southerners tried to organize such a movement, it never gained sufficient momentum to pose a real threat.[350] (*See* also 'Fort' Riley)

Walker Lake
Mineral County

First visited by Joseph Walker in 1833, this large natural lake bears his name today. On 24 November 1845, Captain John Charles Fremont, U.S. Topographical Engineers, used Walker Lake as a rally point during his return to the east from California.[351]

In April and May 1861, nearly 1500 Paiutes gathered at the mouth of the Walker River. Chief Wahe, supposedly second, only to Old Winnemucca, among the Paiutes planned to take over the Indian agency and then, through apparent peaceful infiltration, attack Fort Churchill. Among the Indians' gathering were Bannocks from Idaho and Oregon and Paiutes from throughout Nevada and adjacent areas. Warren Wasson, Indian Agent for Nevada, went to the gathering accompanied by several Indians who had visited larger settlements in California and knew more of the greater strength of the whites. The wisdom of the other Indians prevailed and Wahe, his plan thwarted, left with the Bannocks.[352]

In early 1862, because of military activities in the Owens Valley in nearby California, Walker Lake Paiutes were concerned about possible hostilities in their area as well. On 27 March, Warren Wasson, accompanied by First Lieutenant Herman Noble and fifty soldiers from Company A, 2nd California Cavalry, met tribal leaders and convinced them that war was not in the best interest of either the whites or the Indians. After Wasson's departure Wahe returned to Walker Lake and again tried to rally support for war. Unable to desuade him, two other Paiute chiefs killed him. To counter Wahe's claim that he was a spirit chief and would return from the dead, the two chiefs cut his remains in small pieces and distributed them in widely separated places. Peace became the way of the Walker Lake Paiutes.[353]

In March 1865, two prospectors, Isaac Stewart (twenty-six years old from Cleveland, Ohio) and Robert Rabe (thirty years old from Germany), were attacked in their camp on the shore of Walker Lake. Rabe, after being shot in the back, was killed by having his head crushed with a large rock. Stewart was scouting the area on horseback when Rabe was killed. When Stewart returned to the campsite the Indians chased him. He rode into the lake in an attempt to escape, but drowned instead. Word of the deaths reached Fort Churchill and, on 11 March, Captain William Wallace was tasked to apprehend the murderers. His force was a composite of thirty-seven soldiers from Company A, 1st Nevada Infantry, and fifty soldiers under Lieutenant William H. Clark from Company E,

1st Nevada Cavalry. Tribal leaders from the Walker Lake reservation were cooperative. By the 15th the two Indians responsible were identified and quickly located. When they were captured they offered to ransom their ponies and if that was not enough they offered that their fathers be hanged in their place. The two were taken first to Fort Churchill and then to Aurora where they were turned over to civilian authorities.

Reports vary on whether they escaped or were turned loose.[354] The pair then killed two friendly Indians. On 1 June Captain Wallace returned to Walker Lake to apprehend them. There he met a large force of well-armed Indians. In a surprisingly bold act he ordered his men to disarm the Indians and then he arrested about 150 of them. Once in control he agreed to release all of them except the brother and uncle of the two murderers. Shortly, one of the murderers was delivered to Fort Churchill. The hostilities in Paradise Valley and along the Humboldt River (*see* Camp No. 16) prevented recapture of the second offender.[355]

Wall Springs
Washoe County

This spring and grove of cottonwood trees were used as a campsite by Lieutenant John Littlefield with a detachment from Company D, 1st Nevada Cavalry, in July 1864, while en route from the Santa Rosa Mountains to Camp Pollock on the Nevada-California boundary. Within the month, he again camped at the site with thirty troopers en route from Honey Lake, California, to Unionville to investigate rumors of Confederate activity there.[356] In March 1865, station owner Lucias Arcularius was killed by Indians at Wall Springs. A month later his station at Granite Creek, a few miles to the east, was also attacked by Indians and the occupants killed. The source for the name of the springs is unknown.

Wall Spring is located on the northern edge of the Smoke Creek Desert. Go north from Gerlach nine miles on State Route 447 and then west on Washoe County road (maintained gravel) nine miles. This site is on private land.

Williams Station and Honey Lake Smith's Station
Lyon County

In 1860, James O. Williams and his two brothers owned and operated this station on the Overland Trail. The brothers held two or three Indian girls at the station against their will. In May, various Indian chiefs from the region met in council near Pyramid Lake to decide for or against war versus conference with the whites to resolve differences. Mo-guan-no-ga, Paiute chief from Big Meadows and later known to the whites as Captain Soo, became impatient with the direction of the council. On the evening of 7 May 1860, he rode with several of his warriors to Williams Station. There he killed two of the Williams brothers and three other whites, burned the station to the ground, and freed the captive Indian girls. In addition to the rescue, Mo-guan-no-ga's intent was to force the intertribal council to a decision in favor of war with the whites.

The next day, James Williams, who was camped a few miles away during the attack, returned to the station where he found the bodies and the smoldering ruins. He immediately went to Virginia City to report the incident. The news of the two attacks precipitated the first battle at Pyramid Lake in which seventy-six members of the one-hundred-and-five white force were killed.[357]

The site of Williams Station is on the Carson River and is now under the waters of Lake Lohanton.

Willow Point, Camp
Humboldt County

Willow Point was a frequent rendezvous site during the 1865 campaigns around Paradise Valley. On 4 April 1865, First Lieutenant Joseph Wolverton was camped here with a twenty-five-man detachment from Company D, 1st Nevada Cavalry. By chance, the civilians evacuating Paradise Valley came upon him. Acting on their information, two days later he engaged and killed ten Indians near the site of an earlier Indian attack. (*See* Cottonwood Creek.) Later that same day he killed two more. Wolverton's only loss in the fighting was one horse.[358]

In late July 1865, R.H. Scott, a rancher in the area, had asked for protection from a band of Indians harassing settlers near Willow Point. The mission was given to ten soldiers from Company D, 1st Nevada Cavalry, under Sergeant David Thomas and twenty-one other soldiers from Company I, 2nd California Cavalry, under Sergeant James F. Stephens and Corporal Charles S. Rugg.[359] On 26 July, Rugg, with six California soldiers and rancher Scott were gathering forage in his field about four miles from the main body. They were confronted by a large band of Indians arriving from the hills to the east. The Indians were posturing for an attack, so Rugg raised a white flag and began talking to them. Scott left immediately to go for help and quickly covered the four miles to where Thomas and eight Nevada soldiers were tending livestock. Five or six civilians and other California soldiers were also summoned back to Scott's field.[360] Including the civilians, the balance of power between the soldiers and the Indians was now about even.

The reinforcing soldiers under Thomas arrived from the east, deliberately cutting off the Indians' escape route into the mountains. The Indians were clearly a part of the war party that days before had been harassing the settlers. Also, only moments before, when the Indians had superior numbers, they had been menacing Scott and the corporal's work party. It is unclear which side fired the first shot, but undoubtedly the soldiers were inclined toward a battle based on these recent events. As the whites advanced, the Indians retreated into the tules and swampy area along the Little Humboldt River. Five Indians ran for cover in a nearby cabin. The cabin was torched and the Indians were killed as they ran out while attempting to escape the flames. A running battle with the remaining Indians followed. It covered several miles and lasted from 2:00 p.m. until darkness. The combined soldier/civilian force killed twenty-one Indians in the fight. Some were known to have escaped across the stream into the nearby hills. Military casualties included Private Augustus S. Herford, killed and Privates Thomas J. Rehil and Joshua C. Murphy, all of Company I, wounded.[361] The civilians lost one killed, Joseph Warfield, and two wounded, Mark W.

Haviland and a Mr. Travis shot in the wrist.[362] Several horses were wounded, including five arrows shot into Thomas' horse.[363]

In August 1865, Major Michael O'Brien of the 6th California Infantry took command of the field operations after the death of Lieutenant Colonel McDermit. He established his headquarters in a semi-permanent camp at Willow Point. Headquarters for military operations in and around Paradise Valley remained at Willow Point through the summer. In October 1865, the command moved to Dun Glen.[364]

To reach Willow Point, go approximately twenty-three miles north of Winnemucca on US Highway 95. Turn east on State Road 290 for slightly over two miles. Turn southeast of Godchaux Road and go four miles to present-day Willow Point (an intersection). The Willow Point of the 1860s was an undefined area along the Little Humboldt River about four miles due east. Nothing remains to mark use by the military.

Willow Springs (Willow Creek Station)
Pershing County

Willow Springs, also known as Willow Creek Station is located on the Honey Lake to Humboldt Road which passes between the Saint Mary's Hotel and Rabbit Hole. On 29 July 1864, a detachment of Company D, 1st Nevada Cavalry, camped here. Second Lieutenant John Littlefield reported, "July 29, left [Trego] Hot Springs at 5 a.m.; arrived at Willow Creek at 6.30 p.m. after a hard drive of forty miles. Hay and good water for stock."[365] Frequent use of the road by troops from Camp Smoke Creek and Dun Glen seemed to maintain order through 1864. In 1865, Paiute Chief Black Rock Tom and his band of renegades from several tribes began raiding throughout the area adjacent to the Black Rock Desert. In November they attacked a teamster, Mr. Bellew, at Cedar Springs (six miles west of Willow Spring) and plundered his wagon. The hapless wagoneer was part of a group of three or four teams and became separated as his team moved ahead of the main party. This and other attacks prompted the cavalry's unsuccessful response a few days later.[366] (*See* Paiute Creek.)

On 13 September 1865, Captain Robert Payne with soldiers from Company E, 1st Nevada Cavalry, attacked an Indian Camp "in Quin's [sic] River Valley on Willow Creek; a running fight ensued that lasted about three hours, resulting in the killing of thirty-one Indians, and wounding of one white man."[367] Payne divided his force into two elements to attack the Indian camp on its flanks. The captain, with nine soldiers and Lieutenant John Littlefield, also with nine soldiers, attacked at daybreak. The Indians retreated quickly, leaving their supplies and equipment. Doubts about Littlefield's courage (*See* Tuscarora Range) were forever removed during the battle. A single Indian, mounted and armed with a spear, charged directly at the lieutenant. Littlefield, "calmly waited until his attacker was at close range and shot him from his horse."[368] It is uncertain if this is the correct Willow Creek, but the evidence and activity of the time tends to support it.

In a less than glorious epilogue, after mustering out ex-Captain Robert Payne "put to good use the knowledge of Northern Nevada he gleaned ... and became a noted cattle rustler in the area."[369] Reportedly he was lured into his crime by the apparently irresistable charms of Susan Warfield Raper. Payne traveled with her through Colorado, Oklahoma, and, eventually, Texas where she left him. She was involved with several frontier men and is a story of her own. An emmigrant from New Zealand, she had at least five husbands (Raper, Booth, Yonkers, Black, and Dawson). One was killed by Indians in Paradise Valley, one she cleaned out and divorced, one she killed (self-defense), one died mysteriously (possibly ingested a toxic substance), and one just left (or did he?).[370] Willow Springs is on the Honey Lake-Humboldt River Road between Rabbit Hole and Saint Mary's Hotel, approximately twenty-five miles west of Exit 145 (Imlay) on I-80.

Zabriskie, Camp

Almost nothing is known of Camp Zabriskie. Neither its location nor its purpose are documented. The only Official Records reference identifies it as a place of assignment for Companies A and B, 1st Nevada Cavalry, in October and November

1863.[370] The dates coincide with the movement of these two companies from Fort Churchill, Nevada, to Camp Douglas, Utah, via the Overland Trial. Conflicting reports of the location place it both twenty-five miles north of Fort Churchill and twenty five miles north of Camp Ruby. It is possible that the reference in the Official Records was either a deception for the eyes of Confederate sympathizers or merely a convenient reference to temporary campsites used by the units during their march to Utah. Records show that Captain Noyes Baldwin was in command of Companies A and B during their march to Utah. It appears that Baldwin was responsible for moving the mounted soldiers while Captain Elias B. Zabriskie was responsible for moving the wagons carrying the supplies and company equipment. This was a common separation of duties during an administrative move and accounts for the changing location of Camp Zabriskie. The trains, being slower than the mounted soldiers, were routinely loaded first and put on the road ahead of the main party. In the event of an unexpected attack the better armed and more mobile mounted soldiers were only a short distance behind the wagons and thus available for quick response and pursuit.

Zabriskie was one of the first officers to be accepted for service in the newly authorized Nevada Cavalry. When he joined the regiment he was the District Attorney for the Third Territorial District Court in Nevada. He recruited and formed Company A, 1st Nevada Cavalry in July 1863. Both Companies A and B were recruited from the Virginia City-Gold Hill area and trained at Fort Churchill. Their officers were certified in July 1863. After a short stay at a temporary site near Fort Churchill they were assigned to duty at Camp Douglas, Utah. They left the Carson River area on 29 September, and traveled along the Overland Trail, until they reached Camp Douglas on 21 November 1863. In Utah, they were placed under the command of Colonel (later Brigadier General) Patrick Edward Connor, 2nd California Cavalry and 3rd California Infantry. Zabriskie later became the Judge Advocate for Brigadier General Connor when he was given command of the Department of the Plains in Denver, Colorado.[371]

ENDNOTES

Endnotes

[1] Helen S. Carlson, *Nevada Place Names*, pg. 39.

[2] Frank A. Root and William Elsey Connelley, *The Overland Stage to California*, pg 103.

[3] Dorothy Mason, *The Pony Express in Nevada*, pg. 58.

[4] *Ibid.*

[5] *Ibid.*, pg. 43.

[6] Herbert M. Hart, *Old Forts of the Far West*, pg. 184

[7] U.S. War Department, *The War of the Rebellion, A compilation of the Official Records of the Union and Confederate Armies*, Chapter LXII, p.148. (Hereafter referred to as *Official Records.*)

[8] Myron Angel (ed.), *History of Nevada*, pg. 166.

[9] Richard H. Orton, *Records of California Men in the War of the Rebellion 1861-1867.* (Hereafter referred to as Orton, *Records of California Men.*) Private Spratt recovered from his wound and mustered out of the service on 27 September 1864.

[10] Angel, *History of Nevada*, p. 166.

[11] *Ibid.*

[12] *Official Records,* Chapter LXII, p. 1119.

[13] *Ibid.*

[14] Phillip D. Smith, *Nevada Historical Society Quarterly*, "Sagebrush Soldiers, Nevada's Volunteers in the Civil War," p. 50. (Hereafter referred to as "Sagebrush Soldiers.")

[15] *Official Records,* Chapter LXII, p. 148.

[16] Carlson, *Nevada Place Names*, p. 43.

[17] Smith, "Sagebrush Soldiers," p. 50.

[18] *Ibid.*, p. 40.

[19] *Ibid.*, p. 52.

[20] *Ibid.*

[21] *Ibid.*, p. 40.

[22] *Ibid.*, p. 67.

[23] *Ibid.*, p. 73.

[24] *Ibid.*, p. 72.

[25] Hart, *Old Forts of the Far West*, p. 70.

[26] Robert W. Frazer, *Forts of the West*, p. 90.

[27] *Official Records,* Chapter LXII, p. 773.

[28] Hart, *Old Forts of the Far West*, p. 70.

[29] Carlson, *Nevada Place Names*, p. 45.

[30] Smith, "Sagebrush Soldiers," p. 45.

[31] Sessions Wheeler, *The Black Rock Desert*, p. 128.

[32] *Humboldt Register*, 20 January 1866.

[33] Wheeler, *The Black Rock Desert*, p. 132.

[34] Orton, *Records of California Men*, p. 187.

[35] *Ibid.*, muster records.

[36] *Humboldt Register*, 20 January 1866.

[37] Angel, *History of Nevada*, p. 175; Wheeler, *The Black Rock Desert*, p. 123; and Hubert Howe Bancroft, *The Works of Hubert Howe Bancroft, Volume XXV, History of Nevada, Colorado and Wyoming 1540-1888*, p. 220.(Hereafter referred to as Bancroft, *History of Nevada*.)

[38] *Humboldt Register*, 27 January 1866.

[39] Carlson, *Nevada Place Names*, p. 47.

[40] Bancroft, *History of Nevada*, p. 206.

[41] Hart, *Old Forts of the Far West*, p. 184.

[42] *Ibid.*

[43] *Ibid.*

[44] Angel, *History of Nevada*, p. 150.

[45] Orton, *Records of California Men*, p. 85.

[46] Raymond M. Smith, *Nevada's Northwest Corner, The Black Rock Country of Northern Humbodlt, Pershing & Washoe Counties*, p. 47. (Hereafter referred to as Smith, *Nevada's Northwest Corner*.)

[47] Wheeler, *The Black Rock Desert*, p. 121.

[48] Angel, *History of Nevada*, on page 174, reports the arrest site as Humboldt Sinks and the captor as Indian Captain Soo. Richard H. Orton, *Records of California Men in the War of the Rebellion 1861-1867*, on page 186, reports the arrest of Black Rock Tom at 'Blake's Station.' Sessions Wheeler, on page 123, quotes the 30 December 1865 *Humboldt Register* identification of the arresting officer as a Captain 'Steele' with the arrest taking place at Big Meadows. Review of the California muster rolls shows no Captain Steele. However, there is a Captain Harlow L. Street who was assigned to Company K, 2nd California Cavalry, at the time that Black Rock Tom was arrested. Given that the records were handwritten it is likely that Captain Steele was in fact Captain Street. After mustering out of the California Cavalry, Captain Street was accepted into the 1st U.S. Cavalry as a first lieutenant. He remained in the service until 1 January 1871. Blake's Station is on the west side of the Humbolt River adjacent to mile marker 109 on I-80.

[49] Hart, *Old Forts of the Far West*, p. 184.

[50] Carlson, *Nevada Place Names*, p. 53; Hart, *Old Forts of the Far West*, p. 184; and Roberts, *Encyclopedia of Historic Forts, The Military, Pioneer, and Trading Posts of the United States*, p. 492. (Hereafter referred to as Encyclopedia of Historic Forts.)

[51] Francis B. Heitman, *Historical Register and Dictionary of the United States Army*. (Hereafter referred to as Heitman, *Historical*

Register); and "Report of the Secretary of War to the House of Representatives, Second Session of the Fortieth Congress, 1867-68, p. 148.

[52] Carlson, *Nevada Place Names*, p. 61.

[53] Dorothy Mason, *The Pony Express in Nevada*, p. 14.

[54] *Ibid.*, p. 48.

[55] *Ibid.*, p. 49.

[56] *Ibid.*, p. 48.

[57] Dennis G. Casebier, *No. 2, Arizona Monographs,* "Camp El Dorado, Arizona Territory; Soldiers, Steamboats, and Miners on the Upper Colorado," p. 25. (Hereafter referred to as Casebier, "Camp El Dorado.")

[58] Hart, *Old Forts of the Far West*, p. 184.

[59] Angel, *History of Nevada*, p. 172.

[60] Smith, "Sagebrush Soldiers," p. 46.

[61] Roy S. Bloss, *Pony Express - The Great Gamble*, pp. 4-6.

[62] Carlson, *Nevada Place Names*, p. 70; and Hart, *Old Forts of the Far West*, p. 184.

[63] Mason, *The Pony Express in Nevada*, p. 10.

[64] Hart, *Old Forts of the Far West*, p. 184.

[65] Smith, "Sagebrush Soldiers," p. 10.

[66] *Ibid.*, p. 19.

[67] *Official Records,* Chapter LXII, p. 1080.

[68] Smith, "Sagebrush Soldiers," p. 42; and *Official Records,* Chapter LXII, p. 1275.

[69] William F. McConnell, *Journal of the Council on America's Military Past, Volume XIII, Number 4,* December 1985, "Nevada's Lost Civil War Post," pp. 143-145.

[70] Mason, *The Pony Express in Nevada*, p. 16.

[71] Angel, *History of Nevada*, p. 169.

[72] Smith, "Sagebrush Soldiers," p. 32.

[73] Mason, *The Pony Express in Nevada*, p. 17.

[74] Angel, *History of Nevada*, p. 183.

[75] Robert W. Frazer, *Forts of the West,* p.92; Hart, *Old Forts of the Far West*, p. 48; and Smith, *Nevada's Northwest Corner*, p. 11.

[76] Smith, "Sagebrush Soldiers," p. 79; and Angel, *History of Nevada*, p. 184.

[77] Frazer, *Forts of the West*, p. 92.

[78] Heitman, *Historical Register.*

[79] *Ibid.*

[80] Bloss, *Pony Express - The Great Gamble*, p. 74.

[81] Mason, *The Pony Express in Nevada*, p. 21.

[82] Angel, *History of Nevada*, p. 169; and Hart, *Old Forts of the Far West*, p. 49.

[83] Bloss, *Pony Express - The Great Gamble*, p. 30.

[84] Angel, *History of Nevada*, pp. 170-171; and Smith, "Sagebrush Soldiers," pp. 64-65.

[85] Angel, *History of Nevada*, p. 170.

[86] Smith, "Sagebrush Soldiers," p. 66, quoting the *Reese River Reveille,* 28 April 1865. A.P.K. Safford and W.R. Usher are listed as privates on the muster roles of Company A, Humboldt Guards. Neither Bonnifield nor Parkinson are listed in the muster roles of the militia.

[87] Jay Henry White, *History of the Nevada Militia, 1862-1912,* Humboldt County, The Buena Vista Guards, Cavalry.

[88] Smith, "Sagebrush Soldiers," p. 66.

[89] *Ibid.*, p. 75.

[90] Casebier, "Camp El Dorado," p. 27.

[91] Mason, *The Pony Express in Nevada*, p. 11.

[92] Bancroft, *History of Nevada,* p. 181.

[93] Smith, "Sagebrush Soldiers," p. 41.

[94] *Official Records,* Chapter LXII, p. 380.

[95] Carlson, *Nevada Place Names*, p. 94.

[96] *Official Records,* Chapter LXII, p. 1279.

[97] Carlson, *Nevada Place Names,* p. 97; and Mason, *The Pony Express in Nevada*, p. 38.

[98] Angel, *History of Nevada*, p. 169.

[99] Wheeler, *The Black Rock Desert*, p. 118.

[100] Mason, *The Pony Express in Nevada*, pp. 29-30. Other spellings include Rosier, Losier and Loscier.

[101] Angel, *History of Nevada*, p. 177. Angel used the nickname 'Little Baldy' for Lafayette Bolwinkle.

[102] *Ibid.*; and Mason, *The Pony Express in Nevada*, p. 28.

[103] Mason, *The Pony Express in Nevada*, p. 30.

[104] *Ibid.*, p. 23.

[105] *Ibid.*

[106] Angel, *History of Nevada*, p. 181. Angel reports the Caldwell house in 1881 stood on the site of the battle where Duck Creek opens out in the Steptoe Valley.

[107] Hart, *Old Forts of the Far West*, p. 51.

[108] Smith, "Sagebrush Soldiers," p. 47.

[109] Angel, *History of Nevada*, p. 172; and Hart, *Old Forts of the Far West*, p. 51.

[110] *Official Records,* Chapter LXII, p. 1178.

[111] Smith, "Sagebrush Soldiers," p. 63.

[112] *Ibid.*, p. 64.

[113] *Ibid.*, p. 66.

[114] *Ibid.*, p. 72.

[115] Carlson, *Nevada Place Names*, p. 102; Hart, *Old Forts of the Far West*, p. 51; *Official Records;* and Angel, *History of Nevada*, p. 173.

[116] Orton, *Records of California Men*, p. 185.

[117] Angel, *History of Nevada*, p. 173.

[118] Casebier, "Camp El Dorado," p. 25; and Hart, *Old Forts of the Far West*, p. 51.

[119] Smith, "Sagebrush Soldiers," p. 64; and Angel, *History of Nevada*, p. 173.

[120] Frederick H. Dyer, *A Compendium of the War of the Rebellion*, California and Nevada Units; and Angel, *History of Nevada*, p. 173. (Hereafter referred to as Dyer, *A Compendium.*)

[121] Carlson, *Nevada Place Names*, p. 102; and Hart, *Old Forts of the Far West*, p. 51.

[122] Hart, *Old Forts of the Far West*, p. 184.

[123] Don Ashbaugh, *Nevada's Turbulent Yesterday, a study of Ghost Towns*, p. 188. (Hereafter referred to as Ashbaugh, *Nevada's Turbulent Yesterday.*)

[124] Angel, *History of Nevada*, p. 173.

[125] Heitman, *Historical Register* and Regimental Returns and General Order 33, Department of California.

[126] Carlson, *Nevada Place Names*, p. 105.

[127] Bloss, *Pony Express - The Great Gamble*, p. 97 reports the stationkeeper as Albert Armstrong instead of Mike Holten.

[128] Mason, *The Pony Express in Nevada*, p. 52.

[129] Heitman, *Historical Register.*

[130] *Ibid.*

[131] Mason, *The Pony Express in Nevada*, p. 53.

[132] Mason, *The Pony Express in Nevada*, p. 51; and Ashbaugh, *Nevada's Turbulent Yesterday,* p. 302.

[133] Angel, *History of Nevada*, p. 180.

[134] *Ibid.*

[135] *Ibid.*

[136] *Official Records.*

[137] Hart, *Old Forts of the Far West*, p. 184.

[138] Carlson, *Nevada Place Names,* p. 106.

[139] *Official Records,* Chapter LXII, p. 355.

[140] James R. Hinds, *Journal of the Council on America's Military Past, Volume XVII, Number 2, April 1990*, "The Army and Las Vegas: A Century of Association," p. 37. (Hereafter Hinds, "The Army and Las Vegas.")

[141] Casebier, "Camp El Dorado," p. 2.

[142] *Ibid.*, p 34.

[143] *Ibid.*, p. xx.

[144] Hart, *Old Forts of the Far West*, p. 184.

[145] *Official Records,* Chapter LXII, p. 414.

[146] *Ibid.*, p. 1268.

[147] *Ibid.*, pp. 1118-1119.

[148] Heitman, *Historical Register.*

[149] Carlson, *Nevada Place Names*, p. 113.

[150] *Official Records,* Chapter LXII , p. 378.

[151] Bloss, *Pony Express - The Great Gamble*, pp. 99-100.

[152] Mason, *The Pony Express in Nevada*, p. 8.

[153] Carlson, *Nevada Place Names*, p. 118; and Hart, *Old Forts of the Far West*, p. 184.

[154] Mason, *The Pony Express in Nevada*, p. 9.

[155] Smith, *Nevada's Northwest Corner,* p. 45.

[156] Thomas Wilson, *Pioneer Nevada*, p. 105.

[157] Carlson, *Nevada Place Names*, p. 126

[158] Smith, "Sagebrush Soldiers," p. 64.

[159] Angel, *History of Nevada*, p. 178.

[160] Bancroft, *History of Nevada,* p. 219. This order was rescinded in December 1864, when General Irvin McDowell, Commander of the Department of the Pacific, issued an order to field commanders that no Indian who surrendered was to be killed, but rather turned over to civil authorities.

[161] *Official Records,* Chapter LXII, p. 125.

[162] *Ibid.,* p. 149.

[163] Dyer, *A Compendium.*

[164] Orton, *Records of California Men* , pp. 171-172.

[165] William M. Pond, *Journal of the Council on America's Military Past, Volume XVII, Number 2, April 1990*, "The Mysterious Ending of Edward McGarry," p. 55 (Hereafter   referred to as Pond, "The Mysterious Ending of Edward McGarry.")

[166] Orton, *Records of California Men*, p. 184.

[167] Mason, *The Pony Express in Nevada*, p. 32.

[168] Orton, *Records of California Men*, pp. 186-187.

[169] *Ibid.*, p. 187.

[170] Heitman, *Historical Register.*

[171] Hart, *Old Forts of the Far West*, p. 184.

[172] *Ibid.;* and Frazer, *Forts of the West*, p. 193.

[173] Bancroft, *History of Nevada*, p. 220; and Secretary of War Report to Congress I.66, 43rd Congress - 1st Session.

[174] Carlson, *Nevada Place Names*, p. 131.

[175] Hart, *Old Forts of the Far West*, p. 184.

[176] Mason, *The Pony Express in Nevada*, p. 12.

[177] Hart, *Old Forts of the Far West*, p. 184; Robert B. Roberts, *Encyclopedia of Historic Forts, The Military, Pioneer, and Trading Posts of the United States*, p. 492; and Carlson, *Nevada Place Names*, p. 132.

[178] Carlson, *Nevada Place Names*, p. 135

[179] Mason, *The Pony Express in Nevada*, p. 15

[180] Post returns for Camp Dun Glen

[181] Wheeler, *The Black Rock Desert*, p. 120.

[182] *Official Records,* Chapter LXII, p. 413.

[183] Mason, *The Pony Express in Nevada*, p. 41.

[184] Carlson, *Nevada Place Names*, p. 152.

[185] Hart, *Old Forts of the Far West*, p. 70; and Hinds, "The Army and Las Vegas," p. 35.

[186] Hinds, "The Army and Las Vegas," p. 35.

[187] *Ibid.*, p. 36.

[188] *Humboldt Register*, 25 November 1865.

[189] Orton, *Records of California Men*, p. 185.

[190] Angel, *History of Nevada*, p. 174.

[191] *Humboldt Register*, 25 November 1865.

[192] Angel, *History of Nevada*, p. 174.

[193] Wheeler, *The Black Rock Desert*, p. 123.

[194] Returns for Fort Churchill for the 2nd California Cavalry show a Sergeant Alexander Lansdon in "confinement" and then, as a private he received a dishonorable discharge 20 April 1866. No specific reason for the reduction in rank and discharge are given. In addition, there is no record of a Private Moon. There is a Private Wesley M. Moore listed in the unit at the time of the battle. It is likely that Private Moore is the soldier that was wounded.

[195] Angel, *History of Nevada*, p. 174.

[196] *Ibid.*

[197] Orton, *Records of California Men*, p. 186.

[198] *Humboldt Register*, 25 November 1865.

[199] Wheeler, *The Black Rock Desert*, p. 118; and Orton, *Records of California Men*, p. 186.

[200] Wheeler, *The Black Rock Desert*, p. 134.

[201] Heitman, *Historical Register*.

[202] Hart, *Old Forts of the Far West*, p. 184.

[203] Angel, *History of Nevada*, p. 146.

[204] Carlson, *Nevada Place Names*, p. 164.

[205] Wheeler, *The Black Rock Desert*, p. 111.

206 Ibid., p. 110.

207 Hart, *Old Forts of the Northwest*, p. xx; Frazer, *Forts of the West*, p. 92; and Carlson, *Nevada Place Names*, p. 160.

208 Pond, "The Mysterious Ending of Edward McGarry," p. 47.

209 *Ibid.*

210 Hart, *Old Forts of the Far West*, p. 143.

211 *Ibid.*; and Pond, "The Mysterious Ending of Edward McGarry," p. 48.

212 Hart, *Old Forts of the Far West*, p. 143.

213 *Ibid.*, p. 145.

214 Pond, "The Mysterious Ending of Edward McGarry," p. 48; and Frazer, *Forts of the West*, p. 94.

215 Pond, "The Mysterious Ending of Edward McGarry," p. 55.

216 Hart, *Old Forts of the Far West*, p. 144.

217 Carlson, *Nevada Place Names*, p. 161.

218 Hart, *Old Forts of the Far West*, p. 144.

219 Carlson, *Nevada Place Names*, p. 173.

220 Mason, *The Pony Express in Nevada*, p. 47.

221 *Official Records,* Chapter LXII, p. 404.

222 Smith, "Sagebrush Soldiers," p. 61.

223 *Official Records,* Chapter LXII, p. 404.

224 Wheeler, *The Black Rock Desert*, p. 106; and Smith, "Sagebrush Soldiers," p. 62.

225 Smith, *Nevada's Northwest Corner,* p. 12.

226 William F. McConnell, *Journal of the Council on America's Military Past, Volume XIII, Number 4, December 1985,* "Nevada's Lost Civil War Post," p. 40.

227 *Ibid.,* pp. 43-45.

228 Hart, *Old Forts of the Far West*, p. 184.

229 Orton, *Records of California Men*, p. 191.

230 Hart, *Old Forts of the Far West*, p. 51; and Roberts, *Encyclopedia of Historic Forts*, p. 493)

231 Root and Connelley, *The Overland Stage to California*, p. 103.

232 Angel, *History of Nevada*, p. 186.

233 Carlson, *Nevada Place Names*, p. 185.

234 Angel, *History of Nevada*, p. 187.

235 Bancroft, *History of Nevada,* p. 209.

236 Wheeler, *The Black Rock Desert*, p. 116; and Angel, *History of Nevada*, p. 174.

237 Ashbaugh, *Nevada's Turbulent Yesterday*, pp. 189-190.

238 Ibid., p. 189.

239 Ibid., p. 190.

[240] Smith, "Sagebrush Soldiers," p. 46.

[241] Angel, *History of Nevada*, p. 170.

[242] *Ibid.*, p. 170; and Ashbaugh, *Nevada's Turbulent Yesterday*, p. 191.

[243] Smith, *Nevada's Northwest Corner,* p. 46; Smith, "Sagebrush Soldiers," p. 74; and Wheeler, *The Black Rock Desert*, p. 107.

[244] Wheeler, *The Black Rock Desert*, p. 107.

[245] Smith, "Sagebrush Soldiers," p. 73.

[246] *Official Records,* Chapter LXII, p. 1179.

[247] Orton, *Records of California Men*, p. 187.

[248] *Official Records,* Chapter LXII, p. 402; and Smith,"Sagebrush Soldiers," pp. 2-30)

[249] Smith, "Sagebrush Soldiers," p. 46.

[250] *Official Records,* Chapter LXII, p. 379.

[251] Smith, "Sagebrush Soldiers," p. 46.

[252] Angel, *History of Nevada*, p. 150.

[253] *Ibid.*

[254] *Ibid.*, p. 151.

[255] *Ibid.*

[256] *Ibid.*, p. 150.

[257] *Ibid.*, p. 165.

[258] *Ibid.*, p. 150.

[259] *Ibid.*

[260] *Ibid.*, pp. 150-158.

[261] Bancroft, *History of Nevada*, p. 215.

[262] Angel, *History of Nevada*, pp. 159-163.

[263] Smith, "Sagebrush Soldiers," p. 79.

[264] Wheeler, *The Black Rock Desert*, p. 133.

[265] Smith, "Sagebrush Soldiers," p. 15.

[266] Ashbaugh, *Nevada's Turbulent Yesterday,* p. 190; and Angel, *History of Nevada*, p. 169.

[267] *Official Records,* Chapter LXII, p. 379.

[268] Smith, "Sagebrush Soldiers," p. 46.

[267] *Official Records,* Chapter LXII, p. 381.

[270] *Ibid.,* p. 411; and Smith, "Sagebrush Soldiers," p. 74.

[271] Mason, *The Pony Express in Nevada*, p. 24.

[272] Carlson, *Nevada Place Names*, p. 202.

[273] Mason, *The Pony Express in Nevada*, p. 36.

[274] *Official Records,* Chapter LXII, p. 667.

[275] Angel, *History of Nevada*, p. 178.

[276] *Official Records,* Chapter LXII, p. 770.

[277] Dyer, *A Compendium.*

[278] Mason, *The Pony Express in Nevada*, p. 24.

[279] Bancroft, *History of Nevada,* p. 219.

[280] Dyer, *A Compendium.*

[281] Frazer, *Forts of the West*, p. 94.

[282] Dyer, *A Compendium,*; and *Official Records,* Chapter LXII, p. 183.

[283] *Official Records,* Chapter LXII, p. 183.

[284] *Ibid.*, p. 379.

[285] Angel, *History of Nevada*, p. 181; and Bancroft, *History of Nevada*, p. 219.

[286] *U.S. Treaty with the Western Shoshoni, 18 Statutes at Large,* p. 689.

[287] Dyer, *A Compendium*; and Smith, "Sagebrush Soldiers," p. 40.

[288] *Official Records,* Chapter LXII, p. 1103.

[289] *Ibid.,* p. 1104.

[290] Carlson, *Nevada Place Names*, p. 206.

[291] Frazer, *Forts of the West*, p. 92; and Carlson, *Nevada Place Names*, p. 202.

[292] *Official Records,* Chapter LXII, p. 380.

[293] Cadastral Survey Records, BLM at Reno, Nevada.

[294] Mason, *The Pony Express in Nevada*, p. 18.

[295] *Ibid.*, p. 54.

[296] Angel, *History of Nevada,* p. 180.

[297] *Ibid.*

[298] Hart, *Old Forts of the Far West*, p. 184; and Roberts, *Encyclopedia of Historic Forts*, p. 494.

[299] Frazer, *Forts of the West*, p. 92; Carlson, *Nevada Place Names*, p. 247; and Angel, *History of Nevada*, p. 175.

[300] Angel, *History of Nevada*, p. 175.

[301] *Ibid.*

[302] *Ibid.*

[303] *Ibid.*, pp. 175-176.

[304] Heitman, *Historical Register.*

[305] Ashbaugh, *Nevada's Turbulent Yesterday,* p. 196.

[306] Angel, *History of Nevada*, pp. 175-176; and Ashbaugh, *Nevada's Turbulent Yesterday,* pp. 194-196.

[307] Angel, *History of Nevada*, p. 176; and Heitman, *Historical Register.*

[308] *Medal of Honor Recipients 1863-1973*, p. 317.

[309] Frazer, *Forts of the West*, p. 92.

[310] Hart, *Old Forts of the Far West*, p. 184.

[311] *Official Records,* Chapter LXII, p. 412.

[312] Smith, "Sagebrush Soldiers," p. 49.

[313] Mason, *The Pony Express in Nevada*, p. 25.

[314] *Official Records,* Chapter LXII, p. 1275.

[315] Carlson, *Nevada Place Names*, p. 219.

[316] Bloss, *Pony Express - The Great Gamble*, page 103, reports the spelling as 'Cherry.'

[317] *Ibid.*

[318] Mason, *The Pony Express in Nevada*, p. 22.

[319] *Official Records,* Chapter LXII, p. 1139.

[320] Carlson, *Nevada Place Names*, p. 219; and Smith, *Nevada's Northwest Corner,* p. 43.

[321] Smith, "Sagebrush Soldiers," p. 32.

[322] *Official Records,* Chapter LXII, p. 380.

[323] *Ibid.,* p. 1279.

[324] Carlson, *Nevada Place Names*, p. 219.

[325] Pond, "The Mysterious Ending of Edward McGarry," p. 47.

[326] Carlson, *Nevada Place Names*, p. 220; and Hart, *Old Forts of the Far West*, p. 184.

[327] Mason, *The Pony Express in Nevada*, pp. 56-57.

[328] Angel, *History of Nevada*, p. 181; and Bancroft, *History of Nevada,* p. 219.

[329] Angel, *History of Nevada*, p. 183.

[330] Ashbaugh, *Nevada's Turbulent Yesterday*, p. 326.

[331] Smith, "Sagebrush Soldiers," p. 45.

[332] Ibid., p. 63.

[333] *Official Records,* Chapter LXII, p. 1187.

[334] Jay Henry White, *History of the Nevada Militia, 1862-1912,* Humboldt County, The Humboldt Rangers.

[335] Frazer, *Forts of the West*, p. 94.

[336] Angel, *History of Nevada*, p. 162; and Hart, *Old Forts of the Far West*, p. 184.

[337] Mason, *The Pony Express in Nevada*, p. 73.

[338] *Official Records,* Chapter LXII, pp. 379-381.

[339] Angel, *History of Nevada*, p. 168.

[340] Smith, "Sagebrush Soldiers," pp. 57 and 66.

[341] Ibid., p. 67.

[342] *Reese River Reveille,* 28 June 1865.

[343] Smith, "Sagebrush Soldiers," pp. 68 and 74; Wheeler, *The Black Rock Desert*, p. 110; Hart, *Old Forts of the Far West*, p. 50; Carlson, *Nevada Place Names*, p. 160; and Bancroft, *History of Nevada,* p. 220.

[344] *Reese River Reveille,* 25 May 1865.

[345] Smith, *Nevada's Northwest Corner,* p. 46.

[346] Carlson, *Nevada Place Names*, p. 236.

[347] Heitman, *Historical Register*.

[348] *Official Records,* Chapter LXII, p. 511.

[349] Angel, *History of Nevada*, p. 266.

[350] Smith, "Sagebrush Soldiers," p. 42.

[351] Carlson, *Nevada Place Names*, p. 240.

[352] Angel, *History of Nevada*, p. 165.

[353] Ibid.

[354] Smith, "Sagebrush Soldiers," pp. 58 and 60; Angel, *History of Nevada*, p. 169; and *Official Records,* Chapter LXII, pp. 404-405.

[355] Smith, "Sagebrush Soldiers," p. 60; and *Official Records,* Chapter LXII, p. 405.

[356] Smith, *Nevada's Northwest Corner,* p. 46.

[357] Angel, *History of Nevada*, p. 150; Bancroft, *History of Nevada*, p. 208.

[358] Angel, *History of Nevada*, p. 170; and Ashbaugh, *Nevada's Turbulent Yesterday*, p. 191.

[359] Angel, *History of Nevada*, p. 173; and Orton, *Records of California Men*, p. 185.

[360] Smith, "Sagebrush Soldiers," p. 75.

[361] Orton, *Records of California Men*, p. 185.

[362] Angel, *History of Nevada*, p. 173; and Smith, "Sagebrush Soldiers," p. 75.

[363] *Humboldt Register*, 5 August 1865. This account of the Willow Point battle does not match with Myron Angel's account with regard to the names of the wounded civilians.

[364] Angel, *History of Nevada*, p. 173; Hart, *Old Forts of the Far West*, p. 184; Roberts, *Encyclopedia of Historic Forts,* p. 494; and Carlson, *Nevada Place Names*, p. 247.

[365] *Official Records,* Chapter LXII, p. 380.

[366] Angel, *History of Nevada*, p. 174.

[367] Angel, *History of Nevada*, p. 174.

[368] Smith, "Sagebrush Soldiers," p. 80.

[369] *Ibid.*, p. 83.

[370] More can be learned about Susan Warfield in "Susan Raper - Eventful Career," printed in *The Elko Independent*, 6 June 1886, and also in Volume 96, Number 2, of *The Northeastern Nevada Historical Quarterly*.

[371] Smith, "Sagebrush Soldiers," pp. 27 and 53.

APPENDIX A

Chronological Abstract
List of Military Engagements

Chronological Abstract

1776   Fray Francisco Garces travels down Colorado River to California missions.

1826   Jedediah Smith enters Moapa Valley in Southern Nevada.

1827   Jedediah Smith crosses central Nevada.

1828   Peter Skene Ogden explores Humboldt River in Northern Nevada.

1830   Antonio Armijo opens Santa Fe-Los Angeles trade route.

1833   Joseph Walker leads mountain men through central Nevada.

1843   John C. Fremont crosses north-western Nevada.

1848   War with Mexico ends; California and Nevada become part United States.

1849   California population grows from 14,000 Anglo & Hispanics to 100,000;
Mormon Station (Genoa) established.

1855   Fort Mormon (Baker) established in Las Vegas Meadows.

1857   Brigham Young recalls Mormons to Salt Lake City.

1859   Comstock lode discovered in western Nevada;
Genoa to Camp Floyd, Utah (Overland Trail) road survey completed.

1860   Pony Express mail service established;
May 12, Paiutes defeat civilian militia at Pyramid Lake;
July 20, Fort Churchill established.

1861   December, Mormon Fort at Las Vegas designated as Fort Baker.

1862   September 4, Camp Ruby established;
December 15, Camp at Smoke Creek established.

1863   March, Goshute Indian War begins;
Camp at Dun Glen established.

1864   October, Nevada Statehood granted.

1865   March, Anglo-Indian conflicts increase significantly;
May, Indians defeat Cavalry in Tuscarora Range;
August, Camp McDermit established;
November, Camp McGarry established.

1866   April, Camp at Smoke Creek last used by the military;
August, Camp at Dun Glen abandoned;
October, Camp El Dorado established;

1866   December, Camp Scott established;
December, Camp at Fish Lake established.

1867   July, Camp Halleck established;
November, garrison moved from Camp El Dorado to Fort Mojave;

December, Camp at Fish Lake abandoned.
1868   May, Fort Churchill abandoned.
1869   Transcontinental Railroad completed;
       June, Camp El Dorado removed from rolls;
       September, Fort Ruby abandoned.
1871   February, Camp Scott abandoned;
       March, Camp McGarry transferred to Department of the
         Interior.
       June, Fort Churchill transferred to Department of the Interior.
1886   October, Fort Halleck transferred to Department of the Interior.
1889   July, Fort McDermit transferred to Department of the Interior.

List of Military Engagements

(Match with corresponding numbers on map on page 178.)

	LOCATION	DATE	UNIT	COMMANDER
1	Pyramid Lake	2 Jun 1860	3rd US Arty & 6th US Inf., Cos. A & H	Cpt. J.M. Stewart
2	Egan Station	16 Jul 1860	4th US Artillery, Co. B	1Lt. S.H. Weed
3	Gravelly Ford	29 Sep 1862	2nd CA Cavalry, Cos. H & K	Maj .E. McGarry
4	Duck Creek	4 May 1863	2nd CA Cavalry, Co. K	Cpt. S.P. Smith
5	Spring Valley	5 May 1863	2nd CA Cavalry, Co. K	Cpt. S.P. Smith
6	Cherry Creek	Aug 1863	3rd CA Infantry, Co. E	1Lt. J. Hosmer
7	Disaster Peak	May 1864	2nd CA Cavalry, Co. B	Cpt. T. Ewing
8	Mud Lake	14 Mar 1865	1st NV Cavalry, Co. D	Cpt. A.B. Wells
9	Walker Lake	15 Mar 1865	1st NV Inf., Co. A & 1st NV Cav., Co. E	Cpt. Wm. Wallace
10	Martin Creek Gap	5 Apr 1865	1st NV Cavalry, Co. D	1Lt. W. Wolverton
11	Tuscarora Range	7 May 1865	1st NV Cavalry, Co. D	1Lt. J. Littlefield
12	Tuscarora Range	20 May 1865	1st NV Cavalry, Co. D	Cpt. A.B. Wells
13	Silver Creek	29 May 1865	1st NV Infantry, Co. B	2Lt. J. Tolles
14	Willow Point	26 Jul 1865	1st NV Cav., Co. D & 2nd CA Cav., Co. I	Sgt. D. Thomas
15	Table Mtn.	30 Aug 1865	2nd CA Cavalry, Co. I	1Lt. H.C. Penwell
16	Garvelly Ford	2 Aug 1865	2nd CA Cavalry, Co. B	1Lt. R.A. Osmer
17	Willow Spgs.	13 Sep 1865	1st NV Cavalry, Co. E	Cpt. R. Payne
18	S. of Dun Glen	8 Oct 1865	2nd CA Cavalry, Co. I	1Lt. H.C. Penwell
19	Paiute Meadows	9 Nov 1865	2nd CA Cavalry, Co. I	1Lt. H.C. Penwell
20	Leonard Creek	17 Nov 1865	2nd CA Cavalry, Co. B	1Lt. R.A. Osmer

21	Battle Creek	12 Jan 1866	2nd CA Cavalry, Cos. B & I	Cpt. G.D. Conrad
22	Guano Valley	15 Feb 1866	2nd CA Cavalry, Cos. D & F	Maj. S.P. Smith
23	Paradise Valley	7 Mar 1866	2nd CA Cavalry, Co. I	Sgt. J.T. Brown
24	Long Valley (not shown)	3 Oct 1866	1st US Cavalry, Co. A	1Lt. J.F. Small
25	Eden Valley	18 Jan 1867	8th US Cavalry, Co. A	2Lt. J. Lafferty
26	Vicksburg Mines	7 Feb 1867	1st US Cavalry, Co. B	1Lt. G.F. Foote
27	Black Slate Mountain	15 Feb 1867	8th US Cavalry, Co. A	2Lt. J. Lafferty
28	South Fork- Owyhee River	23 Mar 1867 Aug 1867 August 1867	8th US Cavalry, Co. A	1Lt. J. Lafferty
29	near Camp Scott	26 Oct 1867	1st US Cav., Co. L & 8th US Cav., Co. A,	
30	Deep Canyon (Camp Scott)	29 Apr 1868	8th US Cavalry, Co. A	1Lt. J. Lafferty

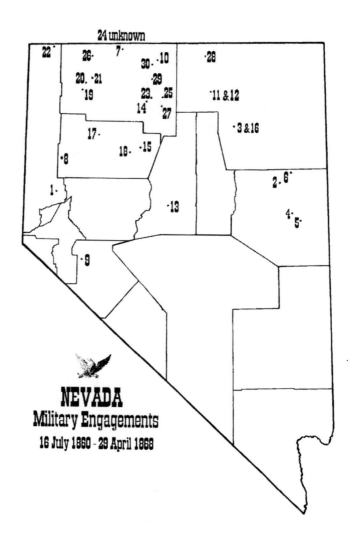

24 unknown

NEVADA
Military Engagements
16 July 1860 - 29 April 1868

APPENDIX B

Early Roads and Trails,
Military Posts and Camps,
and Overland Stations

Early Roads and Trails

AA   Old Spanish Trail
BB   California Emigrant Trail
CC   California Emigrant Trail - Southern Route
DD   Applegate - Lassen Trail
EE   Overland Trail - Pony Express Trail
FF   Noble's Cutoff (Honey Lake Road)
GG   Hastings Cutoff
HH   Chico - Boise Road
II   Reese River Road

Military Posts and Camps

	Fort or Camp	Established	Closed
1	Fort Churchill	July 1860	May 1868
2	Fort Baker	December 1861	April 1865
3	Fort Ruby	September 1862	September 1869
4	Camp at Smoke Creek	December 1862	April 1866
5	Camp at Dun Glen	March 1863	April 1866
6	Camp Nye	October 1864	August 1865
7	Fort McDermit	August 1865	January 1889
8	Camp McGarry	November 1865	March 1871
9	Camp El Dorado	October 1866	November 1867
10	Camp Call	October 1866	November 1867
11	Camp Scott	December 1866	February 1971
12	Camp Fish Lake	December 1866	July 1867
13	Fort Halleck	July 1867	October 1886

NEVADA
Early Roads and Trails
&
Military Post and Camps

East to West List of
Overland Trail Stations

Station Name	Distance to next station
Prairie Gate, UT	18
Antelope Springs	13
Spring Valley	12
Schell Creek	12
Egan (Gold Canyon)	15
Butte	11
Mountain Spring	9
Ruby Valley	12
Jacob's Well	12
Diamond Springs	12
Sulphur Springs	13
Roberts Creek	13
Grubb's Well (Camp Station)	15
Dry Creek	10
Cape Horn	11
Simpson's Park	15
Reese River	12
Mount Airey (replaced Dry Wells)	14
Castle Rock	12
Edward's Creek	11
Cold Spring	10
Middle Gate	15
Fair View	13
Mountain Well	15
Still water	14
Old River	14
Bisby's	11
Nevada	12
Desert Wells	13
Dayton	13
Carson	14
Genoa	11

APPENDIX C

Plats and Maps of Selected
Forts and Camps

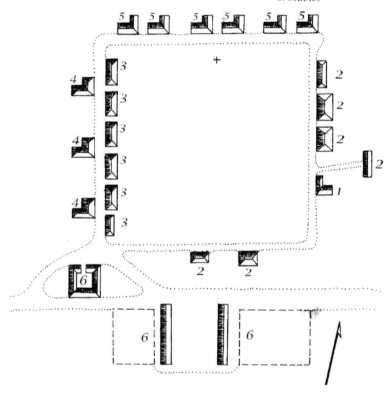

FORT CHURCHILL
NEVADA
1868

1. *Hospital*
2. *Administration,*
   Quartermaster
   & Supply
3. *Company Quarters*
4. *Kitchens*
5. *Officer's Quarters*
6. *Stables*

Fort Churchill Plat

FORT CHURCHILL
July 1860 - May 1868

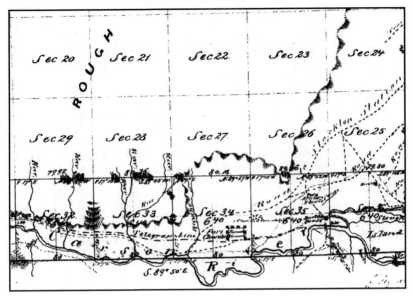

The Telegraph Line and Fort Churchill can be seen in this
land office survey map along the Carson River.
Courtesy: BLM Branch of Cadastral Survey

The Queen of Nevada military posts, Fort Churchill was built of
adobe bricks on rock foundations. Wooden components were
constructed of purchased commercial lumber. Roofs were shingled
with wide eaves and porches were common. Carpenters, masons,
and other professional craftsmen were used in addition to military
labor, making this one of the most expensive western posts to
build. Domestic water was hauled to the site and forage was
obtained from lowland meadows along the Carson River. Fuel
wood was scarce. Anticipating a larger contingent of soldiers, the
post was over built. As a result, it was spacious and comfortable.
Its proximity to a flourishing, but expensive, social environment
in the mining communities to the west, made assignment here more
pleasant than at other Nevada posts. The site is now managed by
the Nevada Division of State Parks.

FORT BAKER - OLD MORMON FORT
December 1861 - April 1865

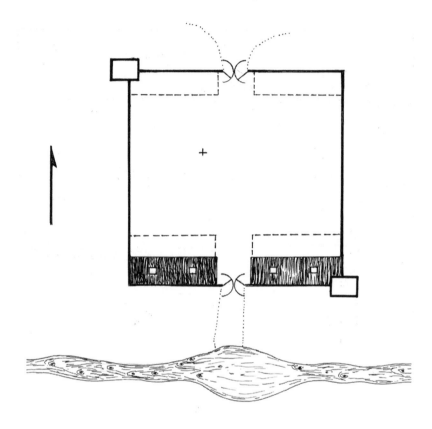

The original structure was built as a fortified Mormon outpost in 1850. Constructed of adobe, this walled fortress enclosed several rooms with sod roofs along its south wall. Materials from the perimeter walls were later used to construct the more traditional dwelling now located on the southeast side of the compound. Water was provided by free-flowing springs to the west and forage came from nearby meadows and cultivated fields. Wood was scarce at this desert post. Today, reconstruction is in progress to restore the essence of the old fort. The site is managed by the Nevada Division of State Parks. This plat of the buildings is patterned after the drawings prepared for John W. Hohmann's report in 1995.

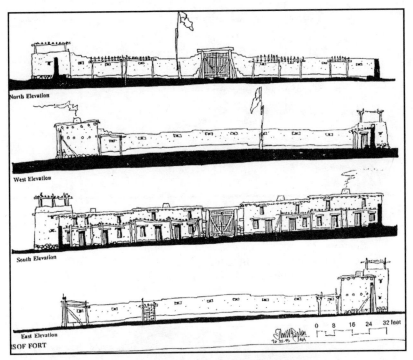

Artist's drawing of interior walls of the
Old Mormon Fort at Las Vegas.
Courtesy: John W. Hohmann, the Louis Berger Group;
drawn by Don W. Ryden, Historical Architect.

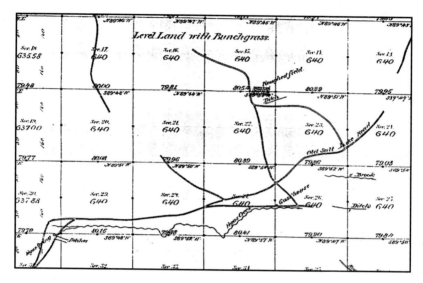

above: An early Land Office map showing Vegas Spring in Section 31
and the Gass' House (Fort Baker site) on the line between
Sections 26 and 27. *Courtesy: BLM Branch of Cadastral Survey*
below: A portion of the most recent USGS 7.5 minute quad sheet.
Fort Baker is southeast of the intersection of Las Vegas Boulevard
and Washington Avenue near the right edge of the map.

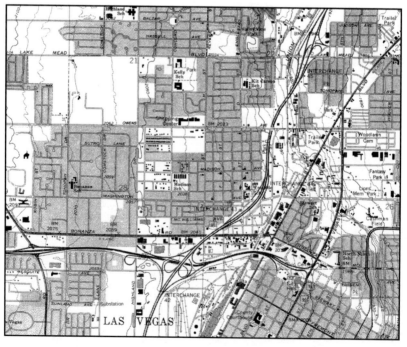

FORT RUBY
September 1862 - September 1869

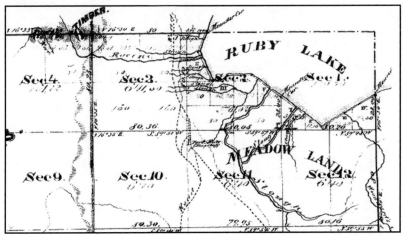

An early Land Office map showing Fort Ruby. The text in Section 11
states, "The Military Post of Fort Ruby is situated in the NQ 1/4 of Sec.
11 and the NE 1/4 of Sec 10, the line between Sect. 10 and 11
running through the parade ground.
Courtesy: BLM Branch of Cadastral Survey

Regarded by many of its occupants as the most miserable post in
the U.S. Army, Fort Ruby was originally constructed entirely of
indigenous materials. Some buildings were stockaded (vertical) log
structures while others used a horizontal log design. Rock fire-
places heated most of the buildings used as offices or as quarters.
In later years, commercial lumber was used as siding material on
the commanding officer's quarters and to replace sod roofs on
dwellings and offices. Water was drawn from nearby springs. Fuel
wood was available in the mountains and native forage was
abundant in meadowlands adjacent to the post. The only known
plat of the fort was prepared by Herbert Hart during his site visit
in the early 1960s. The plat shown below is based on conver-
sations with Hart, as well as interpretation of photographs now
identified as having been taken at Fort Ruby by Timothy O'Sullivan
in 1868. It is possible that other buildings were also used in
connection with the post. Of the original buildings only the stone
building adjacent to the pond is readily recognizable. The site is on
privately owned land.

FORT RUBY
NEVADA
1869

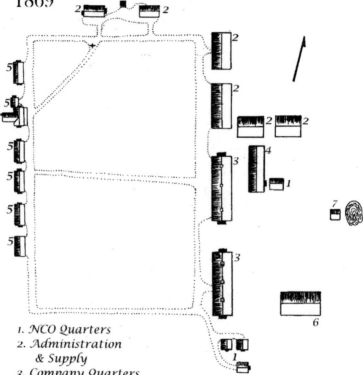

1. *NCO Quarters*
2. *Administration*
   & Supply
3. *Company Quarters*
4. *Kitchen*
5. *Officer's Quarters*
6. *Stable*
7. *Magazine*

Fort Ruby barracks in the foreground showing the stone fireplace, horizontal
log construction and shingled roof. Photograph by Timothy O'Sullivan, circa 1868.
Courtesy: Nevada Historical Society

FORT McDERMIT
August 1865 - July 1889

Fort McDermit photographed from the south
by Timothy O'Sullivan, circa 1868.
Courtesy: Nevada Historical Society

Fort McDermit began as a field camp made up of tents, willow corrals and temporary buildings. A more permanent post was almost immediately constructed using a combination of rock masonry for smaller buildings and frame constructions for barracks and stables. Water was taken from the East Fork of the Quinn River which flows through the post. Forage was available from native range and a hay reserve established to the west. Wood was scarce, but game such as antelope, deer, 'mountain' sheep, sage grouse, ducks, and 'mountain and salmon trout' were common. The plat of the buildings shown below was drawn by Lieutenant George Wheeler during his survey in the later 1860s-early 1870s. Photographs were taken by Timothy O'Sullivan who accompanied Wheeler's party. The site is now part of the Fort McDermit Indian Reservation. Nearly all of the buildings have been dismantled to provide materials for the construction of other facilities needed by the reservation. Only the Adjutant's Office is readily recognizable and is in use today as a community center.

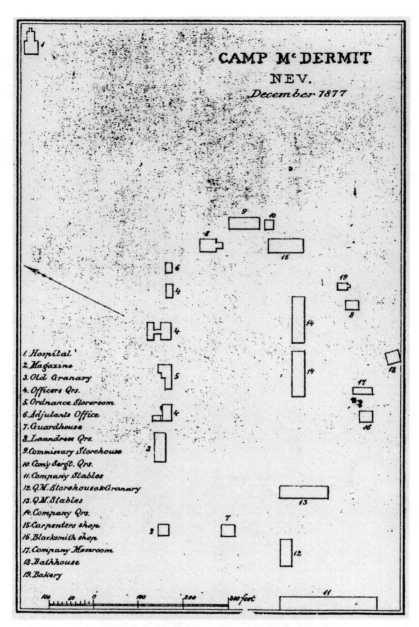

Plat of the Fort McDermit Military Reservation
drawn by First Lieutenant George Wheeler.
*Courtesy: Bureau of Indian Affairs, Phoenix, Arizona,
and the National Archives*

Fort McDermit parade ground looking east with the canyon
of the East Fork of the Quinn River in the background. Circa 1877.
Courtesy: University of Nevada - Reno Library

Soldiers at Fort McDermit. Each strip on the forearm indicates five years of honorable service. Marking above and below the branch insignia on the soldier's cap (behind the cannon) indicate the photograph was probably taken after 1877.

Courtesy: University of Nevada-Reno Library

CAMP McGARRY
November 1865 - March 1871

Conceptual drawing of the east end of the officers' row at
Camp McGarry with the Black Rock Range in the background.
Courtesy: The Author

Camp McGarry was originally comprised of tents and willow corrals.
Eventually rock structures were added. Water came from
Mahogany Creek. Forage was plentiful, but wood was scarce. No
plat or photographs are known to exist for the buildings at this
camp and in some cases the written record contradicts evidence on
the ground today. One reference indicates a stable suitable to
house over 100 horses with a tunnel to the barracks and mess hall.
It is possible that information pertaining to the camp at Soldier
Meadows has been co-mingled with information on Camp McGarry.
Surveyor's notes from 1873 indicate the three foot stub of the flag
pole was used as a survey reference. The drawing below is based
on Herbert Hart's earlier work and recent field observations. The
traditional rectangle and more common alignment parallel to an
adjacent stream channel is inexplicably abnormal. Cursory examination of the soil surface in what would have been the remainder
of the rectangle failed to find any indication of other structures.
The site appears to have been cultivated at one time and surface
evidence may be obscured. The site is now managed as part of an
Indian reservation with administrative offices in Winnemucca.

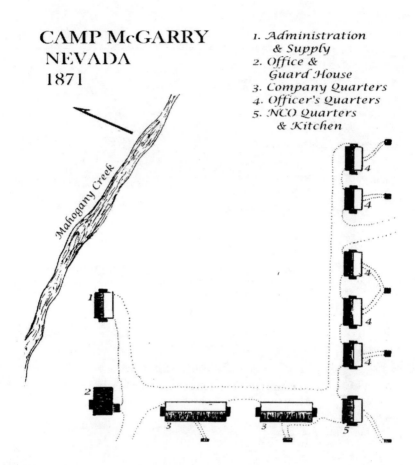

CAMP McGARRY
NEVADA
1871

Mahogany Creek

1. Administration
   & Supply
2. Office &
   Guard House
3. Company Quarters
4. Officer's Quarters
5. NCO Quarters
   & Kitchen

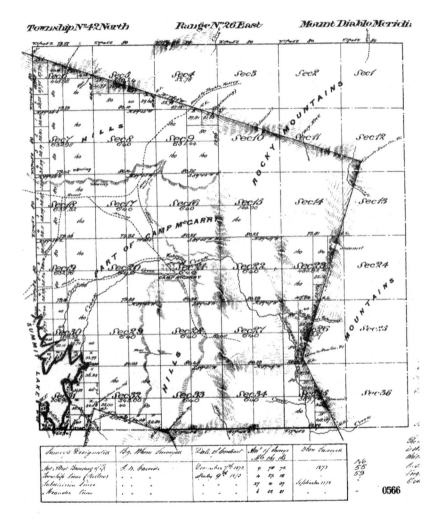

Early Land Office map showing part of the Camp McGarry Military Reservation with a map symbol indicating the location of the post in the NW 1/4 of Section 21.
Courtesy: BLM Branch of Cadastral Survey

CAMP SCOTT
December 1866 - February 1871

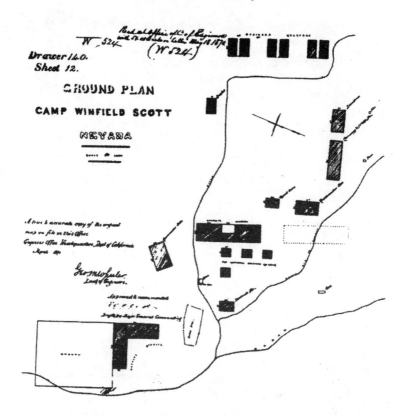

Subordinate to the command at Fort McDermit this post was built in response to the need to curb depredation on farms and ranches in the Paradise Valley area. The post was constructed of adobe with rock foundations. Purchase of 100,000 shingles and 50,000 feet of cut lumber was authorized for construction of roofing material. Beams were to be cut from local timber. Lieutenant George Wheeler mapped the post and prepare the plat seen above. Water was taken from Cottonwood Creek and forage came from adjacent meadows and cultivated fields. Several of the structures still stand today. The site is on private land and is used as the headquarters for a ranch operation. It is not open to the public, however, as part of the Library of Congress American Memory series several of the buildings can be viewed by logging on at http://memory.loc.gov/afc/afc96ran/450.

Between Townships 42 and 43 N. R. 39 E.

West between Sec's 5 and 32

Chains	Va. 18° 15' E.
2.20	Cottonwood Creek. 10 links wide Swift Current. 6 in deep, abound with fine fish. lined by aspen bushes and large willows 2 rods wide — 3 chains below point of Crossing, on the south side of Creek, Scene of the death of James A. Banks Aug. 1st 1867 — Murdered by Indians — from Creek ascend —
12.00	Sum. of South slope of hill, and descend —
18.50	Wood road from upper Cottonwood Creek leading to Camp Scott. and ascend —
40.00	Set a quartzite rock. 15 × 9 × 6 as per instructions. for ¼ sec. cor. Standing on steep East slope, and near Sum. of ridge — from ¼ sec. cor. Military Post bears. S. 49½ E. a Cabin occupied by men, burning
60.00	

This page, taken from the surveyor's notes, states:
"... 3 chains below point of crossing, on the south side of creek,
scene of the death of James A. Banks Aug. 1st 1867 -
Murdered by Indians from creek ascent."
Courtesy: BLM Branch of Cadastral Survey

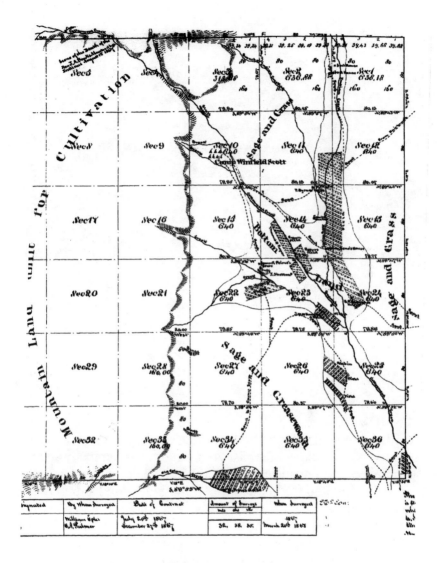

An early Land Office map showing Camp Winfield Scott
in the center of Section 10. The plat also makes a notation
near the top of Section 5 regarding the site where
James A. Banks was murdered in August 1867.
Courtesy: BLM Branch of Cadastral Survey

FORT HALLECK
July 1867 - October 1886

Fort Halleck officer's quarters looking east with the
post hospital in the background.
Courtesy: Nevada Historical Society

As with many posts, initially quarters were no more than
tents. Heavy snows made living difficult at best during winter
months. Stockaded log structures were quickly constructed and
used for storage and as administrative buildings. Eventually adobe
structures were constructed for quarters. The coming of the
railroad facilitated the acquisition of lumber. Wood siding over
the adobe blocks, commercially supplied windows, porches and
shingle roofs gave the post an elegant look. A few frame
buildings were constructed in the later years and used as quarters
for married soldiers. Military demands on the garrison were few
and the handsome appearance made the post an inviting
destination for social activity in the area. Wood and water were
plentiful and forage was abundant on a hay reserve established
for the post. In its later years gardening, sport fishing and
hunting in the nearby Ruby Mountains, as well as an active social
agenda and proximity to the railroad made this an attractive
assignment for married officers.

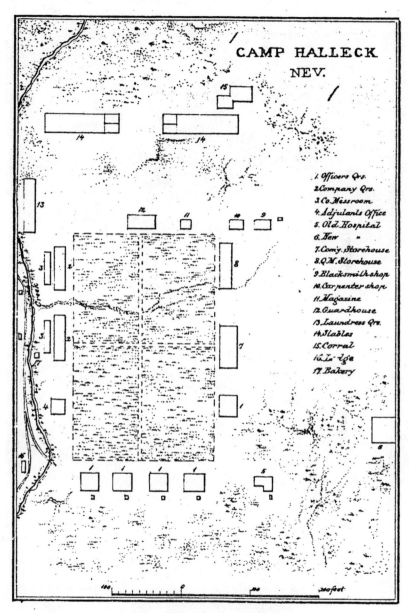

1. Officers Qrs.
2. Company Qrs.
3. Co. Messroom
4. Adjutants Office
5. Old Hospital
6. New "
7. Comy. Storehouse
8. Q.M. Storehouse
9. Blacksmith shop
10. Carpenter shop
11. Magazine
12. Guardhouse
13. Laundress Qrs.
14. Stables
15. Corral
16. Ice Lga
17. Bakery

Ground Plan for Fort Hallack
*Courtesy: Bureau of Indian Affairs, Phoenix, Arizona,
and the National Archives*

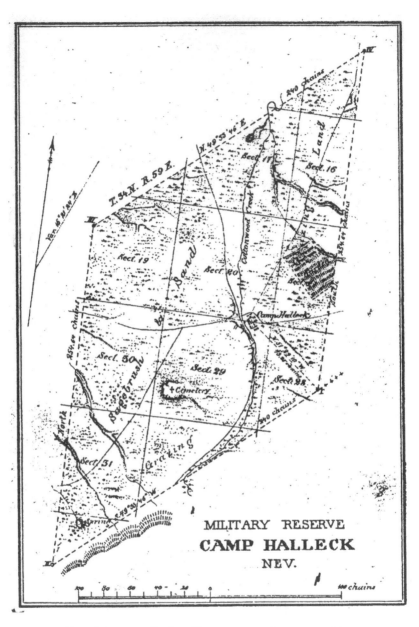

Plat of Camp Halleck Military Reservation prepared by
First Lieutenant George Wheeler.
*Courtesy: Bureau of Indian Affairs, Phoenix, Arizona,
and the National Archives*

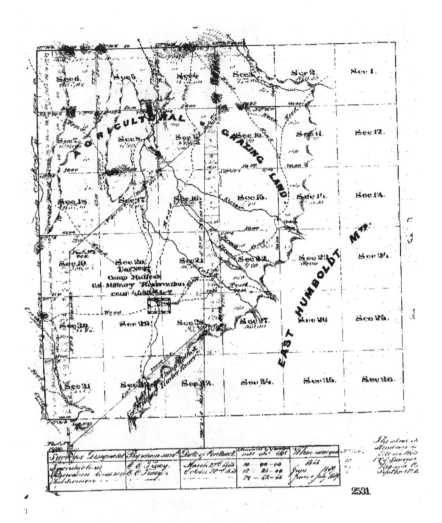

Early Land Office map showing the
Camp Halleck Military Reservation.
Courtesy: BLM Branch of Cadastral Survey

Fort Halleck barracks buildings on the west side of the parade ground looking north toward the stables.
Courtesy: Nevada Historical Society

BIBLIOGRAPHY

Alexander, David V. *Arizona Frontier Military Place Names 1846-1912.* Las Cruces, NM: Yucca Tree Press, 1998.

Abate, Frank R., Editor. *Omni Gazetteer of the United States of America Volume 8.* Detroit, Michigan: Omnigraphics Inc., 1991.

Angel, Myron, editor. Thompson and West. *History of Nevada.* Original, Oakland, CA, 1881. Reprinted Edition, New York: Arno Press, 1973.

Ashbaugh, Don. *Nevada's Turbulent Yesterday, a study in Ghost Towns.* USA: Westernlore Press, 1963.

Bancroft, Hubert Howe. *The Works of Hubert Howe Bancroft Volume XXV, History of Nevada, Colorado, and Wyoming 1540-1888.* San Francisco, CA: The History Company, Publishers, 1890.

Basso, David. *Nevada Historical Marker Guidebook.* Las Vegas, NV: Nevada Publications, 1986.

Bloss, Roy S. *Pony Express - The Great Gamble.* Berkeley, CA: Howell-North Press, 1959.

Boyd, Mrs Orsemus. *Cavalry Life in Tent and Field.* New York: J. Selwyn Tait and Sons, 1891.

Carlson, Helen S. *Nevada Place Names, A Geographical Dictionary.* Reno, NV: University of Nevada Press, 1974.

Carson, Kit. Edited by Milo Lilton Quaife. *Kit Carson's Autobiography.* Lincoln, NE: University of Nebraska Press, 1966.

Coggins, Jack. *Arms and Equipment of the Civil War.* Garden City, NY: Doubleday & Company, Inc., 1962.

Driver, Harold E. *Indians of North America.* Chicago, IL: University of Chicago Press, 1961.

Egan, Ferol. *Sand in the Whirlwind; The Paiute Indian War of 1860.* Garden City, NY: Doubleday, 1972.

Euler, Robert C. *The Paiute People.* Phoenix, AZ: Indian Tribal Series, 1972.

Farrow, Edward S. *Mountain Scouting A Handbook for Officers and Soldiers on the Frontiers.* Norman, OK: University of Oklahoma Press, 1881/2000.

Floyd, Dale E. and the Adjutant General's Office, *Chronological List of Actions, &c., with Indians from January 15, 1837 to January, 1891.* Fort Collins, CO: The Old Army Press, 1979

Frazer, Robert W. *Forts of the West: Military Forts and Presidios and Posts Commonly Called Forts West of the Mississippi to 1898.* Norman: University of Oklahoma Press, 1965.

Gilbert, Bill. *The Trailblazers.* New York, NY: Time-Life Books, 1973.

Goetzmann, William H. *Exploration and Empire - The Explorer and the Scientist in the Winning of the American West.* Austin: University of Texas - Texas State Historical Association, 1993.

Hart, Herbert M. *Old Forts of the Far West.* Seattle, WA: Superior Publishing Company, 1965.

_____. *Old Forts of the Northwest.* Seattle, WA: Superior Publishing Company, n.d.

_____. *Tour Guide to Old Western Forts.* Boulder, CO: Pruett Publishing Co., 1980.

Heitman, Francis B., *Historical Register and Dictionary of the United States Army from Its Organization, September 29, 1789 to March 2, 1903.* Washington, DC: 1903.

Hunt, Aurora. *The Army of the Pacific.* Glendale, CA: Arthur H. Clark Company, 1951.

Irving, Washington. Edited by Edgeley W. Todd. *The Adventures of Captain Bonneville, U.S.A.* Norman: University of Oklahoma Press, 1961.

King, Clarence. *Mountaineering in the Sierra Nevada.* Lincoln: University of Nebraska Press, 1970.

Mason, Dorothy. *The Pony Express in Nevada.* Carson City, NV: Nevada State Museum, 1996 and Harrah's, 1976.

Orton, Richard H. *Records of California Men in the War of the Rebellion 1861 to 1867.* n.p.: 1890.

Patterson, Edna B., Louise A. Ulph, and Victor Goodwin. *Nevada's Northeast Frontier.* n.p.: Western Printing and Publishing Co., 1969.

Patterson, Edna B., and Louise A. Beebe. *Halleck Country, The Story of the Land and its People.* Reno: University of Nevada-Reno, 1982.

Prucha, Francis P. *A Guide to the Military posts of the United States 1789-1898.* Madison: The State Historical Society of Wisconsin, 1964.

Reinfeld, Fred. *Pony Express.* Lincoln: University of Nebraska Press, 1966.

Roberts, Robert B.. *Encyclopedia of Historic Forts, The Military, Pioneer, and Trading Posts of the United States.* New York: MacMillan Publishing Company, 1988.

Root, Frank A. and Connelley, William Elsey. *The Overland Stage to California.* Glorieta, NM: The Rio Grande Press. Inc., 1901 (reprinted 1960).

Simpson, Captain James Hervey. *Report on the Explorations Across the Great Basin of the Territory of Utah for a Direct Wagon-Route from Camp Floyd to Genoa in the Carson Valley, in 1859.* Washington, DC: US Engineers Department, 1876.

Smith, Raymond M. *Nevada's Northwest Corner, The Black Rock Country of Northern Humboldt, Pershing & Washoe Counties.* Minden, NV: Silver State Printing, Inc., 1996.

Stirling, Matthew W. *National Geographic on Indians of the Americas*. Washington, DC: The National Geographic Society, 1955 - reprinted 1965.

Stubbs, Mary Lee and Stanley Russell Conner. *Army Lineage Series, Armor-Cavalry Regular Army and Army Reserve*. Washington, DC: Office of the Chief of Military History, United States Army, 1969.

Townley, John M.. *The Pyramid Lake Indian Wars*. Reno, NV: Jamison Station Press for the Great Basin Studies Center, 1984.

U.S. Adjutant General's Office. *Cavalry Tactics: United States Army, Assimilation of the Tactics of Infantry and Artillery*. D. Appleton and Company, 1876.

U.S. Adjutant General's Office w/introduction by Dale E. Floyd, *Chronological List of Actions, &c., with Indians from January 15, 1837 to January, 1891*. Fort Collins, CO: The Old Army Press, 1979.

U.S. Ordnance Department, *Ordnance Memoranda No. 18.Proceedings of the Board of Officer on Horse-Equipments, Cavalry Equipments and Accouterments, Saddler's and Smith's Tools and Materials, and Standard Supply-Table of Ordnance Stores for Cavalry Service*. Washington, D.C.: U.S. Government Printing Office, 1874.

United States War Department. *The War of the Rebellion, A Compilation of the Official Records of the Union and Confederate Armies*. Washington, DC: US Government Printing Office,
> *Series I, Volume 46, 1895.*
> *Series I, Volume 47, 1895.*
> *Series I, Volume 48, Parts I & II, 1896.*
> *Series I, Volume 49, 1897.*
> *Series I, Volume 50, Parts I & II, 1897.*
> *Series III, Volume 3, 1899.*
> *Series III, Volume 4, 1900.*
> *Atlas and Maps to Accompany the Official Records.*

Urwin, Gregory J.W.. *The United States Cavalry, An Illustrated History*. Poole, Dorset, U.K.: Blandford Press, 1984.

Utley, Robert M. *Frontiersmen in Blue: The United States Army and the Indian, 1848-1865*. New York: The Maximillian Co., 1967.

_____. *Frontier Regulars: The United States Army and the Indian, 1866-1891*. New York:, n.p., 1973.

Webb, George W. *Chronological List of Engagements Between the Regular Army of the United States and Various Tribes of Hostile Indians which occurred during the years 1790 to 1898, Inclusive*. New York, NY: AMS Press, Inc., 1976. (Reprint of the 1939 edition.)

Wellman, Paul I. *Death of Horseback: Seventy Years of War for the American West.* Philadelphia & New York: J.B. Lippencott Co., 1934.

Wheeler, Sessions S. *The Black Rock Desert.* Caldwell, ID: The Caxton Printers, Ltd., 1978.

Wilson, Thomas. *Pioneer Nevada.* Reno, NV: Harold's Club, 1951 and 1957.

Publications

Hinds, James R., "The Army and Las Vegas: A Century of Association." *Journal of the Council on America's Military Past,* Volume XVII, Number 2, April 1990.

McConnell, William F. "Nevada's Lost Civil War Post." *Journal of the Council on America's Military Past,* Volume XIII, Number 4, December 1985.

Middagh, S.H. "Extracts from the Regimental Scrape Book," *The Cavalry Journal,* October 1915 and January 1916.

Pond, William M. "The Mysterious Ending of Edward McGarry." *Journal of the Council on America's Military Past,* Volume XVII, Number 2, April 1990.

Ruhlen, Col. George. "Early Nevada Forts." *Nevada Historical Society,* Quarterly Volume VIII, Number 3-4 1964.

Ruhlen, Col George. "Carleton's Empty Fort," *Nevada Historical Society Quarterly, Volume II, Number 2, Spring 1959.*

Smith, Philip Dodd. "Sagebrush Soldiers, Nevada's Volunteers in the Civil War." *Nevada Historical Society Quarterly, Volume 5, Numbers 3-4 Fall and Winter July-December, 1962.*

Monographs

Casebier, Dennis G. *No. 2, Arizona Monographs* "Camp El Dorado, Arizona Territory; Soldiers, Steamboats, and Miners on the Upper Colorado." Tempe, AZ: Arizona Historical Foundation, December 1970.

Unpublished Manuscripts

Dodson, Edward S. *A History of Nevada During the Civil War,* unpublished Masters thesis, University of Oregon, July 1947.

White, Jay Henry, Adjutant General of Nevada. *History of the Nevada Militia, 1862-1912.* Unpublished MS., Adjutant General's Office. Carson City, NV.

Index